The Psychology of Customer Care

A Revolutionary Approach

James J. Lynch

First published 1992 by
THE MACMILLAN PRESS LTD
Houndmills, Basingstoke, Hampshire RG21 2XS
and London
Companies and representatives
throughout the world

ISBN 0-333-55769-7

A catalogue record for this book is available
from the British Library.

Printed and bound in Great Britain by
Billing and Sons Ltd, Worcester

For Christine

Details of consultancy and training services on 'the psychology of customer care' are available from:

Service Excellence Associates
Lions Green House,
Lions Green,
Heathfield,
East Sussex TN21 OPJ.

Telephone or Fax: 04353 2599

Contents

List of Figures and Tables

Figures

Tables

Preface

The service quality revolution of the 1980s has been superseded by a customer counter-revolution in the 1990s. The result is that *customer care* and *service management* techniques developed in the last decade are outmoded. The compliant consumer has been transformed into the 'discerning demander' seeking instant and continuing gratification of psychological needs as well as product satisfaction.

Many of the customer care programmes of the 1980s were based on quality management techniques developed in manufacturing industries throughout the 1960s and 1970s. They had the merit of heightening awareness in service industries of the importance of the quality dimension as a competitive weapon. Standards of service in airlines, banks, hotels and supermarkets were enhanced, but the *nature* of service remained unchanged; or where it was changed its significance was unrecognised.

In this book I explore the changing universe of service, using universe literally. Customers are now booked on the first commercial flight to the moon; Japanese investors are committed to building a 'resort hotel' in outer space. These plans will become realities within the life-span of readers under 30. But we must avoid star-gazing and focus on the challenging changes facing all service industries on planet Earth:

- The need to integrate the customer, in a positive way, into the process of the service system rather than being treated as external to it.
- The blending of technology and human capabilities to add value progressively to the service experience.
- The development of a language and a repertoire of behaviours which will simultaneously satisfy the physical and psychic needs and expectations of customers.
- The devising of new concepts which reveal the core of the appealing features of existing and emerging services.

We will explore new horizons, some more distant than others, in our quest to transform the 'average customer' into an advocate of service supremacy of businesses in fields as diverse as funeral undertaking, dry cleaning, banking, airlines, hotels and supermarkets, plus more esoteric services such as a 'temps agency' for Roman Catholic priests.

Part I deals with the more tangible and conscious elements which influence customer satisfaction: values and beliefs, age and gender. We consider in detail how best to respond to customer care needs in terms of:

— Life change
— Life enhancement
— Life maintenance.

A variety of ways to influence the satisfaction level of customers are outlined.

Part II covers the key factor which influences all customers – time. Here is explained a revolutionary approach to the use of time as both a product and a service. Sixteen customer time-zones are described and a variety of brand new ways of providing customer care are explained in detail.

Time shaping, time-layering and time-compressing are just a few of the techniques which combine together to provide customer time-care. What is provided is not a new training 'package', but an approach which can be adapted to customer care by any manufacturer or service provider.

In *The Psychology of Customer Care* the reader will find the means, not only of breaking new ground, but of keeping ahead on the shifting sands of change. No matter what the product or service, this book will enable any company which wants to lead in customer care to avoid the fatal embrace of obsolescence and to adopt techniques which will still be novel as we move into the third millennium.

Lions Green   JAMES J. LYNCH
East Sussex

Part I

The Conscious Elements of Customer Care Psychology

1 From Total Quality to Total Care

1.1 INTRODUCTION

Total quality found its finest hour in the 1980s; that hour has passed. This does not mean that there is an inherent fault in the concept of total quality, far from it. Improvements in the function and durability of products over the last decade owe much to the application of statistical quality assurance and other techniques of total quality. The reasons for its obsolescence are that in the 1990s there is a growing need to involve the customer in the processes of manufacturing and, to a greater extent, service industries; companies have to operate as open systems, not closed ones – customers are the new quality controllers.

Total care is not a change of label reflecting a new fashion, a different flavour of the month. The concept of *customer care* grew up in the 1980s as the Siamese twin of total quality, drawing life from the same bloodstream of *top management commitment, zero defects, exceeding expectations.*

The time has come to separate the twins – a delicate operation, but if not carried out it could lead to the demise of both struggling children. For, on closer inspection, total quality and customer care are dissimilar; each has a contribution to make to society, but they are different. Total quality focuses on conformity to predetermined standards; total care focuses on transforming and developing human potential.

1.2 TOTAL QUALITY

Total quality concepts are based on the work of three Americans, J. M. Juran, W. Edwards Deming and Philip B. Crosby. Each worked in manufacturing industries and pioneered techniques of *quality control* drawing on the 'operational research' approaches developed in the Second World War to spur productivity of aircraft, tanks, and telecommunications equipment.

3

The statistical quality control techniques of Deming and Juran caused greater interest in post-war Japan than in their own country. Japan had to restore its industrial infrastructure after the havoc of war. The United States and Britain were too busy satisfying the pent up demand for cars, domestic appliances and a myriad of other goods, to care overmuch about new-fangled ideas of quality. 'Never mind the quality, feel the width' was more than a catchphrase; for many manufacturers it was a philosophy.

In the late 1960s, Japan was becoming a threat to American and European companies; by the mid-1970s it had established itself as a world leader in a wide range of both consumable and capital goods. Increasing numbers of Americans and Europeans drove home in Japanese cars to switch on a Japanese television while eating a meal cooked in a Japanese microwave oven.

Hordes of business executives from Detroit, Coventry, Birmingham, New York and other manufacturing areas rushed to Japan to try to discover 'the Japanese secret'. There was no secret, only a dedication to total quality. The principles underlying this dedication were:

- Full commitment by example from the top.
- A shared awareness of the costs of poor quality.
- Understanding of customers' needs and expectations.
- The setting of specifications, standards and measures to meet customers' needs and exceed their expectations.
- Knowledge of the tools and techniques of total quality.
- The seeking of continuous improvement.
- A belief that everyone in the organisation has a responsibility for quality.

One problem that has haunted total quality is the lack of an agreed definition of 'quality'.

In *Juran on Leadership for Quality* (Free Press, 1989), Juran offers a variety of definitions including 'fitness for use'; 'product features that meet customer needs'; 'freedom from deficiencies'.

Philip B. Crosby, in his book *Let's Talk Quality* (McGraw Hill, 1989) defines *quality* as 'conformance to requirements'. The Crosby Process which has taken hold in many companies is based on 'four absolutes':

(1) The definition of quality is: Conformance to Requirements.

(Quality improvement is based on the principle of getting everything right first time.)
(2) The system of quality is: Prevention.
(We must aim to remove the need for checking and correcting by building in steps which prevent us from doing things wrongly.)
(3) The performance standard is: Zero Defects.
(The standard for everything we do must be to get it right the first time, all the time.)
(4) The measurement of quality is: The Price of Non-conformance.
(Through quantifying the cost of non-conformance we can establish a means of measuring, in financial terms, our quality improvement.)

There can be no doubt that these 'four absolutes' yield excellent results in terms of enhanced quality and cost-effectiveness. However, their roots being manufacturing they do not deal with the psychological impact of good or bad quality on the customer. Furthermore, the Crosby Process, and its many imitators, is primarily designed for a 'closed system' with the customer outside, rather than an 'open system' where the customer is part of the process.

For example, a bank cannot ensure 'zero defects' in processing a loan application if the customer has produced false or inadequate information. Furthermore, if a bank sends out statements to customers who are in credit but the statements show them to be in debit will the 'price of non-conformance' be greater in respect of rich Mr A who is mistakenly shown to be £100 overdrawn or poor Mrs B who is mistakenly shown to be £5 overdrawn?

Another limitation of the total quality approach is that it focuses on only one facet of business activity – the customer as a consumer of goods. In the 1990s, 'the Customer' is also aware of other criteria for selecting a company:

— Environmental responsibility;
— Local community support;
— Ethical behaviour.

A letter which is perceived by the customer as inaccurate, unnecessary or both is judged not only as a sign of bad quality but as a waste of scarce resources.

Customers are adopting a more holistic approach to quality; as the durability of products and reliability of services improve, due to the pioneers of total quality, the customer increasingly is seeking satisfaction of psychological needs, recognition of the need to take account of more than the here and now, and a genuineness in relationships. The customers of the 1990s do not want to be served, they want to be cared for as never before.

1.3 TOTAL CARE

Total quality appeals to the intellect; *total care* appeals to both heart and mind. It is the manifestation of anticipating customer wants and needs, responding to them in a manner which displays concern for their best interest.

By breaking down this definition it is possible to analyse the true essence of total care and its distinction from total quality:

- Total care is the manifestation . . . : Care can be seen, felt, and smelt; there is always evidence that care is or is not present in any given situation.
- . . . of anticipating: practitioners of total care do not await for situations to arise before taking action; they are constantly on the alert, forewarned and forearmed.
- . . . customers' wants and needs: total care does not seek to convert 'wants' into needs which suit the current marketing strategy; it seeks to find out what customers really want and sets about satisfying them in a manner which exceeds expectations. Total care also recognises that customers will have 'needs' which they may not be aware of; here again the aim is to meet those needs in a manner which exceeds expectations.
- . . . responding to them in a manner which displays concern for their best interest; total care recognises that there are situations where customers need education, guidance and forewarning of danger. 'Tough care' may be needed to persuade a customer to embark on or avoid a certain course of action. For example, a doctor shows tough care in making a patient attempt to walk after a hip operation; a banker shows tough care in withholding a loan from a customer who will only sink deeper into debt; an airline shows tough care in refusing to transport a mother in the final weeks of pregnancy.

Total care embraces all customers, be they consumers, employees, suppliers or agents. It relates not only to each customer in terms of interaction with the company, but also in the context of the environment, the local community and ethical behaviour.

CARE can be expressed in many ways. When it comes to caring for the customer there are three components to be taken into account: people, product (or service), and process of delivery.

- For the People component 'care' means:

    Capture hearts and minds.
    Add value to every experience.
    Reach out to help.
    Empower people to show care.

- For the Product component 'care' means:

    Constantly search out customers' needs and expectations.
    Add value greater than competition.
    Renew product through innovation.
    Ensure value for money.

- For the Process component 'care' means:

    Check that the right things are being done in the right way.
    Adjust to meet changing needs.
    Review progress against goals frequently.
    Explore new ways of enhancing customer satisfaction.

- When it comes to Caring for the Environment it means:

    Carefully weigh up ecological consequences of decisions.
    Adopt environmentally friendly practices.
    Recycle wherever possible.
    Encourage everyone to be environmentally aware.

- Similarly, a new meaning can be brought into play when it comes to caring for the local community:

    Check what you can do to be a good neighbour.
    Always remember you're working in someone's backyard.
    Reinforce the community spirit by supporting local causes.

Emphasise community awareness in employees whenever you can.

- In terms of Ethical Care, care means:

  Comply willingly with legal and regulatory conditions.
  Act fairly at all times.
  Respect confidentiality.
  Exhibit ethical behaviour at all times.

By analysing each of these 'meanings' we can display the holistic nature of total care in all its dimensions.

1.4   TOTAL CARE AND THE CUSTOMER

This is the first dimension of total care. As we have seen it has three components:

(1) People
(2) Product
(3) Process

The first requirement of the people component is to 'capture hearts and minds'. Total care is not a technique, it is a way of living. Unless everyone in a company, from chairman to gatekeeper, believes in and practices total care it will not succeed. To capture hearts and minds it is necessary to open them. Trust-building through openness is the first essential of any total care programme. The objectives of such a programme are:

- To make all employees aware that their major concern is to ensure customer satisfaction.
- To make every individual aware of his/her personal contribution to customer care.
- To enhance the attitudes, skills and psychological insights necessary for effective customer relationships.
- To gain commitment to continuous improvement in all aspects of service/product quality and customer care.

The next prerequisite for total care is to 'add value to every experience'. Customers perceive care in little things that affect them rather than big things that affect everyone.

The third condition for total care of people is to 'reach out to help'. This underlines the need for anticipating customer wants and needs. It calls for high levels of competence and confidence on the part of those employees who are asked to 'reach out'. Mistakes will be made, but they can be dealt with in a spirit of caring criticism which is both guiding and supportive. This brings in the fourth injunction – 'empower people to show care'.

Empowerment is a key force in any total care activity. It calls for careful briefing, the regular review of progress and continuing support from managers. Leaving people to 'get on with it' is not empowerment but abdication. Twenty years ago in a book entitled *A Manpower Development System*, I wrote: 'Man is the most versatile resource available to industry, yet many of the existing practices in relation to personnel administration tend to limit rather than release human ability.' How slow we are to learn. But learn we must if customers are to be truly satisfied and industry is to prosper.

People come to a company because they have a want or a need which they believe that company can satisfy. This leads us to the second component of the customer dimension of total care – the product.

'Constantly search out customers' needs and expectations' highlights the importance of market research. Polls, qualitative research, and analysis of complaints and comments all help to provide an insight into what the customer thinks is important. Encouraging 'caring criticism' by customers is a new challenge for industry. It is so simple to be selective in interpreting the views of customers, accepting the complimentary and rejecting the censorious. If market research is to work it must be rigorous in design and interpretation. The findings, however unpalatable, need to be communicated to all employees so that they are aware of the real priorities of the company.

'Add value greater than the competition' – this has been touched on in reference to the people component. Here the focus is on being aware of the real strengths and weaknesses of the competition. The shedding of the blinkers of myth is important. Competitive advantage needs to be identified, acknowledged and, where possible, overcome. A sense of proportion is essential; why try to be a mile ahead of the competition if a few inches will suffice to attract new custom?

'Renew product through innovation' is another way of saying 'constantly strive for improvement'. Improvement need not be in the function of the product or service. It may be in the packaging and/or the process of delivery; alternatively it may be in the manner in which the procuring of the product is financed.

This leads into the fourth aspect of product care – 'Ensure value for money'. The value of anything is always a matter of judgement; but each of us has a sense of what is good value and what is not. In creating a perception of what is good value for money, it is necessary to bring into play a number of parameters by which value is judged:

— *Scarcity value* is a function of the availability of a product or service.
— *Reserve price value* is a function of the ultimate price which the customer is *willing* to pay beyond what he wants to pay.
— *Opportunity foregone value* is the price of other products and services which a customer is willing to forego in order to acquire another product or service.

In total care it is necessary to think of value in psychological as well as financial terms. A person is willing to pay a financial premium in order to experience an emotional premium. For example, the extrinsic value of a wedding ring may be significantly less than its retail price, but if the groom sees his bride's eyes light up on seeing the ring, he is willing to pay for a psychological premium.

The last customer component of total care is the process component. This is where total care comes closest to total quality. 'Checking that the right things are being done in the right way' focuses on conformity to standards. This can best be achieved when employees can see their work in a total care context; people need to understand where they fit into the process if they are to be expected to improve that process. They need to feel that what they are doing is worthwhile if they are to be motivated to do it right. Too often companies induce a 'first time syndrome' in employees, through lack of training and communication:

(a) Every day is a 'first time day' because no learning has occurred on previous days.
(b) Every customer is a 'first time customer' because no records or memories are kept of previous visits.
(c) Every complaint is a 'first time complaint' because no action has been taken on previous similar complaints.

Getting things right first time is a desirable objective, but so is the elimination of the other 'first time' syndrome.

A keynote of total quality is flexibility. Hence, 'Adjust to meet changing needs' is a prescription for survival. The world is constantly changing, posing new challenges, imposing new values, opening new horizons. Customer problems rarely fit neatly into company pigeon holes. Iron-fast conditions of trade shackle potential opportunities for improving business opportunities; the shackles must be split open using the chisel of common sense and care. In the 1990s companies need to adjust to the wants and needs of customers; the reverse spells doom.

In a fast-changing world it is necessary frequently to check one's progress to ensure not only that one is on the right road, but that new roads which spring up overnight do not lend better opportunities for enhanced profit and customer care. Annual stocktaking, annual pay awards, annual performance reviews are outmoded. Review cycles need to be more frequent, the period being dictated by customer needs rather than company reporting calendars. As we shall see in Part II, in terms of total care, timing is of the essence.

'Explore new ways of enhancing Customer satisfaction' lies at the heart of customer care. 'Promises', 'surprises', 'the delight factor', are all expressions of this exploration:

- Promises are specific undertakings to care for customers in a particular manner:
   'Never knowingly undersold'
   'One call does it all'
   'Never more than three at a check-out'.
   These are all examples of simple promises which call into play a range of skills, systems and procedures if the promise is to be kept.
- Surprises are small, unexpected gestures which enhance customer satisfaction:
   A flower presented to each lady leaving a restaurant.
   An apple on the breakfast tray.
   Windshield cleaned while filling the car.
   A free liqueur at the end of dinner.
   Each of these costs little (they can be built into the price), but makes a big impression. The essential thing is to keep them fresh.

This is where the delight factor comes into play. It is the sustaining of the personal touch in ways which delight the customer. This we will explore in greater depth in Part II.

1.5   TOTAL CARE AND THE ENVIRONMENT

From a tiny bead of concern in the 1960s, environmental concern has grown into a many stranded necklace in the 1990s. How companies wear that necklace will either embellish them or strangle them. Table 2.1 (p. 26) shows how a cross section of industries are responding to the need for environmental care. This analysis highlights the consequences for customers, not all of which will be positive.

'Carefully weigh up the ecological consequences of decisions' is the first article of the creed of environmental care. In the 1990s this will not be an aspiration, but an edict as governmental authorities impose ever more rigid rules and conditions on both prevention and cure. This will reinforce the need to 'Adopt environmentally friendly practices.'. Friendliness is a perception by the individual to whom the hand of friendship is being extended. Therefore, it will not be companies who decide what is environmentally friendly but their customers. The slump in sales of tuna fish in the USA, in 1990, was a warning that in an affluent society customers are willing to forego the demands of the palate to preserve the lives of dolphins caught in the tuna nets.

As the 1990s progress, Animal Rights groups, Save the Whale and Dolphin societies will be joined by others to exert influence (not always moral) on companies and their customers. The depletion of forests, problems of toxic waste, and the hazards of radiation will be key topics in school curricula'; an environmentally focused generation will be making most of the buying decisions by the end of the century. Recycling will become a sign of a 'caring company'.

'Encourage everyone to be environmentally aware' will be part of customer education. Care will need to be taken to avoid the lure of the superficial and the gimmick. Going for the enduring and the significant in terms of environmental care will be the hallmark which distinguishes the genuine total care company from the counterfeit.

1.6   TOTAL CARE AND THE LOCAL COMMUNITY

The 'local community' may be a village or a county; it is not differentiated by geographical features but by its interaction with and dependence on the company concerned.

'Check what you can do to be a good neighbour', is symptomatic of the previously mentioned fact that 'care' is what the customer thinks it is, not the provider of the care.

'Always remember you're working in someone's backyard' is a useful reminder that people's lives are affected in some way by what a company does or fails to do. Airport noise, chemical poisoning, fire hazards are among the most obvious dangers to life. But it is the small irritations of sirens, dirty exhaust emissions, obnoxious fumes, which are often avoidable, that most upset people in their 'backyard'.

'Reinforce the community spirit by supporting local causes' need not be a matter of a cash donation. The use of company sports grounds when not needed by employees, advice on advertising an event, carrying advertisements on company transport all cost next to nothing but generate enormous good will.

'Emphasise community awareness in employees whenever you can' has two merits. It communicates to employees that the company believes they have something to contribute to local activities. This enhances self-esteem. Also, by suggesting involvement in local activities, the company is signalling its belief in a balance between work and private life with time for family and the community. In this instance the company is showing 'double-care', covering both employees and the community.

1.7 TOTAL CARE AND ETHICS

One of the major influences on corporate behaviour in the 1990s will be the reinforcement of ethical standards throughout industry. The greedy few of the 1980s overshadowed the ethical many. Now all are paying the price; the guilty behind prison walls, the innocent within a maze of regulations.

'Comply willingly with legal and regulatory conditions' means that, however irksome, it is better all round to be seen to act responsibly – if for no better reason than how else can a company expect responsible behaviour by all its customers?

'Act at all time fairly'; a sense of fairness must be mutual. If one party feels that the other has a sense of injustice, there is a choice:

— Do nothing;
— Add to the injustice;
— Attempt to eliminate the injustice.

A perception of injustice can arise from a misunderstanding of the conditions previously agreed to; ignorance of company practices; a feeling of being pressurised; or a lack of options. Whatever the cause, the service provider should strive to create in the customer's mind a sense of fair play.

'Respect confidentiality' is more important in medical and financial services than in, say, department stores. However, if the customer wants to keep some matter confidential (within the bounds of the law), then it is the responsibility of the service provider to respect the customer's wishes. This can extend to such an apparently trivial matter as not disclosing, even inadvertently, over the phone, details of a surprise when the 'wrong person' answers.

'Exhibit ethical behaviour at all times' is the best way to inculcate ethical behaviour in others. Ethics are the engine of caring behaviour. They enable people to work proudly and be proud. Just as the dirt of unethical behaviour brushes off on those who condone it, so too will the brightness of ethical behaviour shine on those who shelter under its halo.

1.8 CONCLUSION

Total quality has contributed greatly to enhanced standards of products and services. Its disciplines will continue to be necessary if companies are to meet customers' needs for product satisfaction. However, as the variations between price and quality of similar products become negligible, a new differentiating factor comes into play – psychic satisfaction.

Total care will achieve that satisfaction more readily than will total quality. The essence of care is that it comes from the heart as well as the mind. It caters for the emotions as well as the senses; it draws out from people the totality of their human potential, rather than circumscribing them with sterile statistical methods. Computers can monitor quality levels, detect deviations from specifications and set right the action required to provide a product with zero defects.

Computers can calculate infinitely quicker and more accurately than any human, but they do not have the capacity to care; that is the prerogative of humans and animals. However, animals appear to care only for the physical needs of their offspring. What makes mankind unique is the ability to care not just for the physical, but for the psychological needs of fellow beings.

The caring ability of humans has been relatively untapped; social status, racial prejudice, individual introversion, fear of failure, anxiety about doing the right thing, greed, agression, cruelty and indifference have all put up barriers to caring. Unfortunately, many of these will remain but others are being eroded.

Total care is an approach to optimising customer satisfaction and at the same time creating a better world. It is an approach which calls for an understanding of customer psychology – the psychological factors which combine to create in the mind of every customer a sense of satisfaction, a desire to repeat the experience, a determination to give business to those who provide not only desired goods and services but who impart a sense of care.

There are profits to be made by applying the new customer care psychology described in this book. Not only money profits for those who provide goods and services, but life-enhancing profits for all.

2 New Thinking About New Customers

2.1 INTRODUCTION

The customers of the 1990s are different from those of previous decades. This is due to a number of major social, political and economic shifts, which although they have their roots in earlier times are becoming more influential as we approach the new millennium:

- The socio-political world has changed with the end of traditional Communism and the rise of a new consumerism throughout Europe.
- The materialistic values of the 1980s are giving way, particularly in the USA and Britain, to more caring ideals about people and the environment generally.
- Customers, individually and collectively, are becoming aware of their power, reinforced by consumer-biased legislation.
- Service industries are playing a more important role than manufacturing and agriculture in most developed economies.

It is against this background of global change that companies are developing their strategies for capturing and retaining customers. This calls for new thinking on how to optimise customer satisfaction while maintaining profit growth.

From the outset it is necessary to distinguish between the concepts of 'consumer' and 'customer'. A consumer is an individual who may or may not buy a product or service but who disposes of products and services to satisfy a need. For example, a father and children may consume foods which the mother has selected and purchased as a customer. A customer is an individual who makes a conscious decision to purchase a particular good or service in preference to using the purchasing power on alternatives. For example, a mother may decide to purchase cheaper foods in order to buy clothes.

All customers are consumers, but not all consumers are customers; prisoners have to eat and be clothed but they have little say in what they consume.

The critical attributes of a customer are:

— freedom of choice in the purchasing decision;
— conscious exercise of that choice which results in the selection of certain goods and services and the rejection of others;
— involvement at the point of service delivery.

This book focuses on customer care psychology mainly in relation to service industries, being primarily concerned with the factors which lead to customer satisfaction rather than the purchasing process itself. Assuming that the extrinsic values of competing goods and services are equal in price and quality, what are the psychological rather than economic factors which lead to a customer choosing one product or service in preference to another?

The answer lies in a new approach which responds to customers' needs for different types of time. This concept of 'customer-time-care' is explored in Part II.

2.2   THE GROWING ROLE OF SERVICE INDUSTRIES

Service industries are growing across the world. The term 'service' implies the performance of specific functions for individuals; such functions may range from the intangible, such as providing professional advice, to being a channel through which individuals can choose from a variety of tangible goods.

Services can be classified in a variety of ways, a major division being services to individuals and services to industry and government. Our concern is with services to individuals. These we can classify as:

- Financial services
    Banks
    Building societies
    Insurance
    Life assurance

- Travel Services
    Airlines
    Railways
    Car hire
    Airports
    Garages and petrol stations

- Leisure services
  Hotels
  Restaurants
  Cinemas
  Theatres
  Pubs and Clubs

- Provisioning services
  Supermarkets
  Department stores
  Mail order
  Boutiques
  Markets

- Communication services
  Newspapers and magazines
  Telephones
  Television
  Radio

- Convenience services
  Travel agents
  Estate agents
  Hairdressing
  Funeral undertakers
  Dry cleaning
  Fast food

Attempting to classify services highlights certain imprecisions. For example, 'travel agents' might be classified under 'travel' or 'leisure'. I have chosen a category, 'convenience services', to encompass a variety of functions which customers could perform by themselves (excluding certain funeral arrangements). You do not need a travel agent to enable you to travel or an estate agent to sell your house – it is simply a matter of convenience. This sector of the service industries is growing fast, with 'agents' providing everything from arranging your wedding to taking your children on holiday or looking after your animals/house/garden while you are absent.

In *The Competitive Advantage of Nations*, Michael E. Porter suggests that the increasing need for services arises from:

(a) greater affluence;
(b) desire for a better quality of life;

(c) more leisure time;
(d) urbanisation (resulting in the need for such services as security);
(e) demographic changes – particularly the increase in dependency groups such as children whose parents are working and more elderly;
(f) socio-economic changes, such as dual-career families where parents have less time to prepare meals and do housekeeping;
(g) rising customer sophistication;
(h) technological changes such as cellular phones, improved techniques in medicine, greater automation of service delivery.

The prospects for service companies have never been better, but the competition has never been greater. Glittering prizes await those who master the new customer psychology.

2.3 CUSTOMER PSYCHOLOGY: THE BASIC MODEL

Throughout this book I shall refer frequently to three 'customer mindsets' which play key roles in determining customer satisfaction. A mindset is a blend of values, attitudes, assumptions and beliefs which determine the perception of an individual in a given situation. Mindsets vary between individuals and over time.

In customer psychology there are three broad categories of mindsets:

(1) Life changing
(2) Life enhancing
(3) Life maintaining

One of these three is a dominant factor in determining the perception of the customer in any service encounter, i.e. the point of contact between the customer and the provider of the service. Contact can be face-to-face, by telephone or letter. At the time of contact the customer will also be influenced by prevailing social values and individual psychological make-up.

The influence of prevailing social values on customer psychology can be seen in the sudden impact of 'environmental awareness' on buying decisions. 'Customer power' is another critical social value which affects customer behaviour. However, the manner in which it affects an individual and how he or she expresses it will be influenced by their psychological make-up. Extroverts are likely to be more assertive in a service encounter than will be introverts.

There is therefore a need to optimise customer satisfaction to take account of:

— Prevailing social values and viewpoints;
— Individual psychology;
— Dominant mindset.

These points are set out below in Figure 2.1.

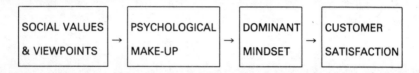

Figure 2.1   The basic model

Identifying the dominant mindset which motivates customer behaviour is one of the key points in customer care psychology.

The life change mindset is associated with important events in life, such as getting married, buying a house, taking a new job, or retiring. Whatever the cause, a life change involves adopting new roles and discarding old ones. This can lead to feelings of confusion, vulnerability and fear. The customer seeking the assistance of a service provider in coping with a life change has very special needs as we shall see in Chapter 4.

The life enhancement mindset is associated with life events which embellish our life-style, such as going on holiday, buying a new car, having a family celebration. Such events can vary significantly in time, cost and numbers involved.

The life maintenance mindset is associated with mundane activities which must be undertaken in order to survive from day to day. These range from shopping for groceries to cashing cheques, paying bills, eating, washing and the like.

The satisfaction of the customer is determined by the degree to which the service provider matches the mindset of the customer. For example, a business person may eat at the same restaurant every day.

Some days, eating alone and in a hurry, the dominant mindset is 'life maintenance'. Other days, eating with a loved one to celebrate an anniversary, the dominant mindset is 'life enhancing'. Finally, there may be a day when the meal is with a potential business partner and the dominant mindset is 'life changing'. It is possible that on each occasion the customer orders a similar meal. The restaurateur as service provider may see his role as providing meals; but in each situation the customer is using different criteria to assess satisfaction.

For life maintenance, speed of service may be an important criterion. For life enhancement privacy and relaxed but attentive service are likely to displace speed. On the rare occasion when a meal is associated with a life change, in the above example the customer may be judging satisfaction in terms of service that boosts self-esteem, permits the display of *savoir-faire*, and is at a pace suitable for the customer's guest.

What may be accepted by the customer as a warm, welcoming gesture in one mindset, may be perceived as overfamiliarity in a different mindset. This and many other aspects of customer mindsets are discussed in subsequent chapters.

2.4   NEW SOCIAL VALUES AND VIEWPOINTS

Social values are deeply held beliefs which influence customer behaviour and choice. Such values would relate to the respective roles of men and women in society. While we accept men as couturiers, female customers, at least in the United States and Britain, would prefer to be served by women when buying a dress. Similarly, male customers prefer to have their hair attended to by a man (as increasingly do women who frequent hairdressing salons).

It takes a long time for a value to take hold, but once embedded it is very difficult to shift. Social values have a bearing on such aspects of customer service as:

- Opening hours;
- Use of credit;
- Race of service providers;
- Use of convenience services such as 'dating agencies' and 'wedding arrangers';
- Attitudes to, and of, service providers;
- Environmental awareness.

Let us consider the impact of these values on customer psychology. Opening hours, particularly shops opening on Sundays, can rouse passions in certain segments of society. Admittedly, some hours are governed by law, but a law can only operate when it is backed by social consensus. Over the past ten years we have seen in the United States, Britain and Western Europe a change in this social value – it is being gradually supplanted by a new social value which might be called 'Any time, any place'. The reasons for this shift in Britain are:

(a) More women at work need access to shops at weekends.
(b) Large chain stores out of town have given non-church attenders a place for family outings on a Sunday.
(c) Punishments for breaking the laws on opening hours are minimal.
(d) Trade unions have become weaker in enforcing their rules, especially on part-time workers.
(e) Technology in terms of TV shopping (on satellite and cable TV) and in 'direct' banking is reinforcing the concept of 'Any time, any place'.

The use of credit to finance consumer durables was much longer taking root in Britain than in the United States, and is still frowned on in many European countries. This social value is undergoing change as credit is used not only to finance tangibles such as cars, but also intangibles such as holidays. However, a distrust of using credit still has roots in Britain, which have sunk deeper with the imposition of charges for credit cards and the development of two-tier pricing. The latter brings to the customer a stronger realisation of the true cost of credit than does a monthly statement of charges. Companies sensitive to the delicate balance of this social value are developing effective means of influencing the customer such as:

- Offering 'interest free' credit on cars and consumer durables – the real cost of the borrowing being covered by a lack of discount in the pricing.
- Providing reductions of up to 5 per cent on restaurant bills settled in cash rather than credit – this 'discount' is covered by making the meal prices inclusive of service and VAT.
- Providing interest or repayment 'holidays' for the first few months after purchase – recouping the 'lost' interest at later stages.

As personal indebtedness increases there is a danger in offering credit for services such as holidays. Having 'consumed' the service customers become disenchanted at having to continue to pay off their loan. The decision in 1990 by Lloyds and Barclays banks to impose an annual charge on credit cards resulted in a total of 1 million customers cutting up their cards. This was because many of the million felt that they were being 'punished' for settling their accounts by the due date, thus not incurring interest charges. At a stroke the banks sent a confusing psychological message to their most creditworthy Customers, implying that the bank would prefer them to be in debt. Coming at a time when all banks were complaining about the failure of businesses and less-developed countries to meet their debts, prudent customers became aware that they were subsidising their spendthrift neighbours. (It was ever thus in banking, but bank managers kept it a well-hidden secret.)

One social value which has undergone change in the past twenty years in Britain is our attitude to the different races in society. Following mass immigration in the 1950s and 1960s black and Asian people tended to work in low-prestige jobs – the major exception being nurses and doctors in the National Health Service. With access to further education, and prodded by legislation, Afro-Asians now permeate virtually all services from TV news presenters to newsagents, from bus drivers to pilots. There are, however, a number of services where the racial mixture is low. Few black or Asian bank managers, estate agents or funeral directors exist outside areas where ethnic minorities dominate.

There are, of course, some services where people of Afro-Asian origin predominate – 'small corner shops', London Underground station staff, nursing orderlies. One might seem to be stating the obvious by claiming that Chinese are dominant in Chinese restaurants, Indians in Indian restaurants and Italians in Italian restaurants. However, this does raise an important point for customer psychology – a Chinese restaurant in which the staff were Italian and vice versa could cause customers some unease. This is not a reflection of racial prejudice, though it may arise from racial stereotyping. Rather it highlights the need for congruity in providing a service. For some time to come, people will prefer to deal with 'their own kind' in certain service encounters. This is particularly true in those services catering for life changes such as weddings and funerals where deep-set cultural taboos prevail. Service providers must, of course, avoid prejudice, but they owe it to their customers to ensure that the racial mix of their staff will add value to the service encounter rather than confuse the customer – otherwise the service will decline.

One part of the service sector which is growing is the 'convenience agency', which ranges from dating agencies to funeral undertakers, from gardening contractors to hospitality consultants. Social values and viewpoints on the acceptability of such convenience agents are changing particularly among the middle and working classes. With more women at work there is a greater willingness to use convenience services.

Another reason for the growth of convenience services is that many of them require little capital to set up; some can be run from home and even be combined with other activities. Car boot sales, for example, can be organised very cheaply, necessitating merely rent for the use of land, a few posters, and telephone contact with a number of potential sellers. For a small outlay it is relatively easy to recoup the costs by charging fees to both sellers and prospective buyers. On the other hand, a home catering service can entail significant costs to meet regulations on hygiene, transport of food, and provision of food, crockery and cutlery.

As convenience services grow, an increasing number of people are becoming service providers as well as customers. This is having an impact on the attitudes to and of service providers. When in the role of service provider a person is put under pressure by customers, then he or she in turn will be inclined to put other service providers under pressure when in the role of customer. A Mori poll, in 1989, found that in Britain 18 per cent of those polled had complained to a shopkeeper in the previous year. Only 9 per cent had gone further and urged others to boycott a particular good or service, while 6 per cent complained to a Citizens Advice Bureau or an independent ombudsman. Whereas in the past a strong social value in Britain was 'not to make a fuss', inhibitions are being broken down with the help of customer-biased legislation, increasingly active consumer action groups, increased awareness of customer rights prompted by television and radio programmes and the press. The propensity to complain to or take some form of action against service providers will increase. Service companies need to prepare their staffs in how to anticipate customer reactions and, above all, how to take preventive action by being more familiar with customer psychology.

Perhaps the most startling change in social values and viewpoints, one which will have an increasing influence on customer psychology, is 'environmental awareness'. Table 2.1 shows some of the action being taken by service industries and their implications for customer care.

Generally speaking, action taken by technology based services (such as airlines) is likely to lead to higher prices. This presents both the customer and service provider with a problem, since there is as yet insufficient evidence as to the trade-off point at which price sensitivity or any other factor will overcome the environmental sensitivity of the customer. Much will depend on his or her psychological make-up.

2.5 THE PSYCHOLOGICAL MAKE-UP OF CUSTOMERS

Regardless of their social values and viewpoints, each customer brings to every service encounter the same components in terms of psychological make-up; though the balance and blend of these components will vary between individuals, and in the same individual over time.

Our aim in this section is to consider only those psychological attributes which are brought into play in service encounters. These are:

(a) Needs
(b) Perceptions
(c) Beliefs
(d) Attitudes
(e) Values
(f) Self-image
(g) Expectations
(h) Feelings

Needs are the prime activators of customers; they are shaped by perceptions and goals. Needs fall into two categories in terms of customer psychology. Physiological needs relate to the tangible aspects of service, such as food, clothes, cars, accommodation. Psychological needs relate to intangible aspects of service, such as comfort, reassurance, security, self-esteem.

Some physiological needs of customers stem from such innate factors as hunger, cold, illness or death. Others are stimulated through advertising, marketing and social pressures. For example, hunger can be satisfied by basic foods, many of which need not be cooked. However, food manufacturers strive to convince customers that their particular brand of food, prepared in a particular manner, is likely to satisfy hunger more effectively than other foods.

Table 2.1 Services industries and the environment

Industry	Action on environmental issues	Benefit for environment	Consequences for customers
Airlines	Change to big fan engines	Less noise Less pollution Slower depletion of fossil fuel reserves	Higher fares due to cost of new aircraft
	Devising corporate policies on environment protection Appointment of senior executive to develop and implement environmental protection policies	Heightens awareness of individual responsibilities	Need to be more litter conscious on board aircraft
	Use of reusable crockery and cutlery	Reduces demand for plastic	Lower standards of trayware, especially on short journeys
	Use of recycled paper and packaging	Reduces demand for timber	
	More use of non-toxic materials for aircraft cleaning and maintenance	Less pollution	Need to use alternative and slower carriers
	Restrictions on haulage of toxic materials	Less hazard due to escape of toxic materials into the environment	
Hotels	Devising corporate policies on environmental issues	Heightens awareness of individual responsibilities	Needs to be more litter conscious in hotel room
	Recycling glass Separating rubbish	Saves raw materials	
	Fine tuning of heating and air conditioning systems	Preserves fuel	May reduce 'personal controls' for heating and air conditioning
	Using household products free	Reduces CFCs	

	Practice	Environmental benefit	Consumer implication
	from CFCs Recycles oil and other materials		Increased tolerance for 'less attractive' toilet paper
	Computer paper recycled and used as writing pads Use of organic vegetables	Preserves forestry Reduces use of chemical fertilisers	Increased tolerance for lower standard of note paper Higher prices
	Use of CO_2 and halon fire-fighting equipment	Reduction of CFCs	
Car hire	Use of lead-free petrol in all cars Use of non-toxic cleaning materials	Reduces lead pollution Reduces pollution	Lower mileage costs
Banks	Credit card subsidy for environmental causes Use of recycled paper	Provides increased funds for projects Saves timber	Allows customer to have choice of charity Increased tolerance for low quality paper
	Sponsorship of special projects	Provides funds for small projects	Increased costs
Supermarkets	Stocking of environmentally friendly brands Use of recycled materials	Reduces pollution Saves timber	Higher prices Cynicism arising from perception of environment issues being exploited for commercial means
	Sponsor environmental awareness campaigns Refusal to stock items involving cruelty to animals	Heightens awareness of environment	Restricted choice

Hunger can also be a psychological need, be it for social recognition, reinforcing self-esteem or other factors which motivate us to choose one service provider rather than another. Table 4.1 (p. 64) shows some of the needs which individuals bring to various service industries. Needs motivate customers, perception shapes their choices of how best to satisfy their needs; expectations help determine how appropriate was the choice.

Perception is not a passive registering of events and people in a service encounter, it is the result of *active thinking* about the service encounter and the customer's involvement in it. In a sense, the customer *constructs* the service encounter. A vital part of perceiving is the attribution of *meaning* to what we experience. The quality of a service encounter will be in some way unique to the customer because its meaning is an outcome of the interplay between the present service encounter and our past experience.

Reality is perception in the sense that our mind shapes our experience by drawing on what it has learned over the years and uses it to recreate our inner world to interpret what is happening in the outer world. Although for purposes of exposition I have listed perceptions, beliefs and attitudes separately, all three interact concurrently in shaping the customer's view of reality.

Beliefs are things we take to be true and treat as facts. In terms of customer care psychology, they stem from both our own direct experience as customers and what we learn from others, such as other customers and the media. As customers we hold beliefs about an enormous number of things. Some of these sets of beliefs that have a marked effect on our perceptions and behaviour as customers are:

(a) Beliefs about the industry we are dealing with.
(b) Beliefs about the service provider.
(c) Beliefs about what should be the respective roles of the customer and service provider in a service encounter.
(d) Beliefs about our rights as customers.
(e) Beliefs about the relationships between behaviour and results, in the sense of 'If, in this situation, I do this, the effect will be that'.
(f) Beliefs about 'pay-offs', that is the likelihood of achieving satisfaction of my needs as a result of taking a particular course of action or behaving in a certain way.

These beliefs guide customer behaviour and the assessment of customer satisfaction by determining our attitudes.

Attitudes are, basically, the stances we take towards something or somebody, in terms of favouring or not favouring, liking or not liking. An attitude is a predisposition to approach a particular service provider on the one hand, or to avoid on the other. Investment in product design, packaging, and customer care training can be wasted by an action which results in the customer adopting a negative attitude.

Values in terms of their social dimension have been previously discussed. They are deeply held beliefs about what is important, good and bad, right and wrong, desirable and undesirable. They provide the criteria which customers use to make choices in selecting a service provider. In addition to the already mentioned social values, there are other 'value clusters' which affect customer psychology:

— Moral values – usually linked to religious beliefs;
— Political values – usually linked to a political party or doctrine;
— Professional values – linked to membership of a particular profession and its code of behaviour.

Self-image is the picture a customer has of himself or herself. It consists of such factors as:

(1) Appearance
(2) Personal manner
(3) Value of job
(4) Relationship skills
(5) Social awareness
(6) Sexual attraction
(7) Self-awareness

Self-esteem lies at the core of self-image. Any action which increases the self-esteem of the customer will raise the level of satisfaction. Damage to self-esteem will have the opposite effect, but to a more intense degree. For most customers the 'added value' resulting from enhanced self-esteem is more difficult to achieve than is the 'negative value' resulting from damage to self-esteem. This is due to the fact that 'personal insecurity' is more prevalent than 'personal security'. People are more willing to believe any confirmation of their own assessment of self-worth than they are to accept a contradiction of it. Conveying in a sincere manner the message 'You are better than you think you are' is a powerful tool for any service provider.

But as with other powerful tools, it has to be handled competently or it may damage its user as well as others present.

Expectations are assumptions about the likelihood of a future event occurring, but with the conscious recognition that there is some degree of uncertainty about the outcome. Customers act on the basis of expectations. They wait for a plumber because they expect he will come as promised, but their values and beliefs are not damaged when he fails to arrive since they have built the 'uncertainty factor' into their psyche. It is this elasticity of expectations which provides a powerful influence in determining customer satisfaction. If the service provider meets the expectation of the customer this has a neutral effect of the level of satisfaction; if the service provider fails to meet the expectations of Customers the effect on satisfaction will be negative; where the expectations of customers are exceeded, even marginally, this has a positive effect on customer satisfaction. Hence the old adage 'Underpromise and overdeliver'.

The cynical reader may feel that there are times when service providers meet the negative expectations of customers, or in other words 'live down to expectations'. Assuming customers are operating in a free market such a state of affairs is unlikely to prevail due to competition. Even in a monopoly market history shows that failure to meet reasonable expectations of customers ultimately results in privatisation, revolution or some degree of substitution.

The final component in the psychological make-up of a customer is possibly the most important in any service encounter – feelings. Strictly speaking, *feelings* are physiological as well as psychological. They can be felt in the mind in terms of fear, grief, anger or happiness, but they are expressed physically by such actions as crying, shouting, laughing or by other body signals. Feelings have their roots in the past; they can easily be reactivated by similar experiences in the present. As customers we recognise this reactivating phenomenon by avoiding service providers with whom we have had a 'bad' experience ('I don't want to go through that again') and returning to those with whom we have had a good experience ('I always feel happy dealing with them').

One of the secrets of effective customer care psychology is to lock into the 'feelings' of customers and massage their psyche in a manner which will help them to enjoy positive feelings or at least to submerge negative ones. Table 4.5 (p. 74) repeats the commonest ways in which customers explain their feelings about service encounters. The vital fact for the service provider is that in each expression of bad feelings there is a clear indicator of how to avoid such feelings recurring in other service encounters. Similarly, in the positive statements there are indicators of what needs to be done to reinforce positive feelings.

Feelings are a key element in determining customer satisfaction in dealing with any service industry. This is because a service encounter is a real time experience which cannot be exactly reproduced due to the dynamics of the relationship between the customer and the service provider. Feelings need to be handled right 'first time, every time' since every service encounter is in some aspect or other a 'first time experience' for both customer and service provider.

2.6 THE ARENAS OF CUSTOMER SATISFACTION

There are four arenas:

(1) Product satisfaction
(2) Peripherals satisfaction
(3) Ambience satisfaction
(4) Psychic satisfaction

Service quality leadership is the prize for whomsoever maximises satisfaction in all four arenas.

Figure 2.2 illustrates the four inseparable arenas relating to any service industry.

The first arena – product satisfaction – covers whatever is the product which the customer has purchased from the service provider.

I PRODUCT SATISFACTION	III AMBIENCE SATISFACTION
II PERIPHERALS SATISFACTION	IV PSYCHIC SATISFACTION

Figure 2.2   Arenas of customer satisfaction

This may be as tangible as a can of beans or as intangible as life assurance. No matter what the product it is essential that it meets the following criteria in the eyes of the customer:

- It performs (or will perform) the function for which it has been purchased.
- Its performance is comparable to or exceeds that specified for products of similar price and availability.
- It meets the physical needs of the customer in a manner which exceeds expectations.
- Any deviations from performance standards will be dealt with in a manner which is acceptable to the customer at the time of purchase.
- The product conforms fully to legal and regulatory requirements. (These criteria can be adapted to intangible products.)

If for each criterion we allocate a satisfaction rating of nought to five then the nearer the score is to twenty-five the higher is the level of satisfaction. But even a twenty-five score in this arena will not in itself be a guarantee of complete satisfaction. Service products are usually easy to copy and difficult to patent. Any bank can readily outmatch a rival's savings or be emulated, at least in its physical aspects, by another; there is little to choose in physical terms between established scheduled airlines flying the same routes with the same frequency at the same fares. This moves us into the next arena of satisfaction.

The second arena – peripherals satisfaction – is a favourite competitive battlefield of many service Industries. Recognising that product satisfaction criteria are difficult to maintain as a basis for differentiation, there is a move to compete on peripherals to the core product. Airlines offer 'free' drinks on every flight, banks offer 'free' insurance cover with every mortgage, hotels offer 'free' fruit baskets, hairdressers 'free' shampoos. An important aspect of this arena is the rise of incentive schemes relating to customer purchases. Vouchers for air flights, hotel nights or theatre visits abound. Associated with this are significant awards for customer loyalty such as TV sets, leather bound books and other glittering prizes.

Less obvious peripherals are the device of clubs by airlines and hotels, membership of which provide exclusive privileges such as quick check-ins and check-outs, priority baggage handling, special lounges at airports away from the hoi polloi.

Peripherals appeal to customer care psychology in terms of enhancing self-esteem ('You're special') and a natural desire for free gifts. However, they can have adverse effects. There is a limit to the amount of free alcohol anyone can drink on a flight. Besides, health conscious customers will have read of its adverse effects resulting in dehydration as well as intoxication. In an age of growing ethical awareness, does the TV set awarded for forty business flights belong to the air-weary employee or the company who paid for all those tickets? When the business traveller goes on holiday with his three noisy children do you let the family use the club lounge and disturb hard-working executives, or do you let him suffer in the air terminal and risk losing his custom. Finally, if the rewards for using a service are extrinsic to it, does this imply that there are no ways in which the quality of the service itself can be improved.

Slowly but surely, customers are beginning to realise that the cost of peripherals are rising and the money is coming from one source – the customer. Another shadow on this arena is what might be called the 'Prince and Pauper syndrome' of 'rewards' which are subject to space availability. This has recently been experienced by passengers of United States airlines who accumulated vouchers for 'free flights' based on the number of miles they had flown paying full fare. First Class and Business Class passengers accumulated free flight entitlements swiftly, but found that when they cashed them in with some airlines they were on a stand-by basis and treated accordingly. This move from being treated as a prince to being treated as a pauper had an adverse effect on their perceptions of the airline. For many the free flight was their last flight with that carrier.

Peripherals which will enhance customer satisfaction should meet five criteria:

(1) They add value to the core product.
(2) They do not damage the health of the customer or induce the customer to do so.
(3) They do not present the customer with ethical dilemmas.
(4) They do not add to the cost of the purchase price of the core product.
(5) They do not lead to the inconveniencing of other customers.

Examples of typical practices by service providers which do not meet those criteria are drawn from airlines:

- Aer Lingus provided every passenger who paid full fare on Dublin–London flights with three bottles of good French wines. This added nothing to their basic product – flying passengers between Dublin and London. In fact their system of cabin service for the majority of passengers followed a sequence whereby those served first with food were served last with drinks. (This may have saved expenditure on in-flight alcohol!)
- All airlines other than those of strict Islamic countries offer more than sufficient amounts of alcohol to passengers. The urge to overindulge is further stimulated by videos and advertisements in their magazines emphasising the low cost of duty free liquor.
- SAS and British Airways in 1990 introduced a range of 'gifts' which in the case of Britain needed clearance by the Inland Revenue because of their benefit in kind. The only qualification for the gifts was undertaking a specified number of First Class or Business Class flights. Gifts ranged from books and children's games to colour TV sets. The tickets were paid for by companies; the beneficiaries were employees who may have been tempted to rearrange itineraries to the disadvantage of their employers in order to qualify for the gifts.
- Some airlines impose an annual charge for the use of lounges by customers who are already paying premium fares.
- Aer Lingus's 'frequent travelling scheme' – entitling the passenger to an award of wine – has to be registered through special computer equipment, thus increasing the time for check-in, resulting in other passengers being delayed.

These are not intended to be carping criticisms of what some service providers may perceive as their generosity. It simply reflects my view that peripherals are, at best, a diversion of attention from the realities of customer care psychology, at worst, they are a 'cop out'.

Once again a naught to five rating by the service provider against each criterion, even if it produced a 'twenty-five' result, would not assure true customer satisfaction. Indeed, a service provider who assessed its peripherals higher than its core product would be in trouble.

Peripherals are likely to be transitory and their absence should not adversely effect the core product. However, they do create expectations and there should be consistency in their availability or fair warning of when they will cease. For example, if a hotel provides its guests with a free morning paper on one visit, the customer may expect to receive the same on a subsequent visit and be disappointed when it does not arrive. It can happen that the withdrawal of a peripheral will cause a greater degree of dissatisfaction than its availability provides satisfaction.

A final aspect of peripherals is that after a time they become in the mind of the customer part of the core product. Meals on short haul journeys by air, tea and coffee making facilities in hotels, bags for groceries are all examples of peripherals which customers take for granted. Their absence is a cause of dissatisfaction whereas their presence is unlikely to add significantly to customer satisfaction.

More difficult to measure is the third arena – ambience satisfaction. Ambience is a blend of tangible and intangible factors which influence the customer's experience in the service encounter. Decor, layout, signposting, furniture, temperature, humidity, appearance of staff, aromas, and music are all tangible aspects of ambience. They can be seen, touched, heard or smelt. All of them provide signals which enter the psyche of the customer and determine satisfaction. Take, for example, sounds; music that is too loud or too frantic can reduce the satisfaction of the customers; indecipherable tannoy announcements particularly at stations and airports are especially annoying; constant staff announcements in stores are distracting; the banging of kitchen doors, slamming of crockery and cutlery and the noise of washing machines are all sounds which destroy the romantic atmosphere of an anniversary dinner. These and less tangible factors are listed in Table 4.3 (p. 67).

Intangible aspects of ambience cover such factors as the disposition of staff, the way in which rapport is established, the manner in which customers are passed from one member of staff to another, the way in which customers are made to feel at ease with their surroundings.

The five criteria which should govern ambience are:

(1) It adds value to the core product;
(2) It is designed to put the customer at ease;
(3) There is a synchronising of the physical design, furnishing and appearance of staff;
(4) Layout, furnishings and such ancillary devices as lifts, escalators and mobile walkways are designed for customer convenience;
(5) Cleanliness, security and accessibility are clearly given special attention.

Examples of lack of attention to these criteria abound. Banks often do not offer sufficient space for privacy; seats in restaurants can be uncomfortable and too close together, thus inhibiting discussion. Well-designed reception areas are spoiled by unkempt staff; customers are required to walk further than necessary because entrances and exits are separated for no apparent reason. Waiting areas in stations, airports and hotels have insufficient seating; signs are inadequate, badly sited or confusing – Euston station in London had a ticket office for 'Suburbs and Outer Suburbs only' leaving the customer to determine where outer suburbs end and somewhere else begins.

It is recognised that ambience is not completely under the control of the service provider: health and safety regulations have to be obeyed; the noise of the aircraft has to be endured; customers can spoil matters by throwing litter, being unkempt and badly dressed. However, the service provider can control most threats to a desired ambience by:

- *Communication*: notices apologising for any inconvenience caused by conforming with national or local laws.
- *Regulation*: stating clearly that persons of a certain age or under-dressed will not be admitted to the premises.
- *Inspection*: having regular routines for checking the state of toilets, fitting rooms and other areas liable to be abused.

As with the two previously mentioned arenas of satisfaction, ambience can to a large degree be measured by both customers and service providers. The last arena – psychic satisfaction – can only be assessed in terms of results by the customer, although the service provider can assess inputs to the creation of such satisfaction.

Psychic satisfaction with service is the arena in which the battle for customer attraction and retention will be fought in the 1990s and beyond. It is the arena with scope for almost infinite expansion, limited only by the capabilities of the mind.

Some individuals in life, generally, are easier to satisfy than others. This is due in large measure to their personality. Stable extroverts do not so readily experience extremes of emotions as do neurotic introverts. An extrovert is easier to satisfy because he or she takes credit for his or her good experiences and blames circumstances for any bad experience. Depressed people, on the other hand, will be more prone to find fault with others.

Certain nationalities reveal wide variations in levels of satisfaction.

The findings of surveys can give a jolt to the traditional stereotyping. Denmark and Sweden register far higher levels of general satisfaction, whereas Italy is the least satisfied nation in Europe. Top of any international listing in happiness is the United States, followed by Australia with Denmark, Sweden and Britain. At the bottom of the developed world are the Japanese.

These international variations provide the backdrop against which the psychic satisfaction of an individual as a customer is determined. The most important factors in influencing psychic satisfaction are:

— Expectations
— Self-esteem
— Goal achievement
— Reduced anxiety

We considered expectations and self-esteem earlier in this chapter and will now deal with the other factors.

A human being differs from other creatures by being a goal-setting and achieving animal. Day in and day out we set ourselves goals ranging from the banal – 'clean the car for the weekend' – to the magnificent – 'will graduate, get married and embark on a career by the time I'm 25'. Whatever their magnitude, however long their time-span, no matter what they demand of us, all goals as customers will be of three basic types:

(1) Life changing
(2) Life enhancing
(3) Life maintaining

We may find that a service provider cannot help us achieve our goal because it is unrealistic, unlawful or in some way undesirable. Possibly the role of the service provider is to help the customer redefine a goal, reassess a target date, renegotiate a deal. Bankers often find themselves in this situation, but so too do:

(a) The clothes department assistant helping the customer to cope with the consequences of putting on weight;
(b) The waiter advising on a menu;
(c) The travel agent suggesting the rescheduling of an itinerary;
(d) The doctor prescribing a new drug;
(e) The petrol pump attendant suggesting a short cut;

(f) The taxi driver recommending a club for a night out with the boys.

In every case where a service provider has an opportunity to influence the goal setting of the customer he or she should grab it, in this way they can better manage the customer's expectations. The smaller the gap between positive expectations and reality, the greater will be the level of psychic satisfaction.

The other gap which the service provider needs to close is the anxiety gap. Anxiety is a feeling of unease about some real or imagined future event. For most customers there will be a correlation between the nature of their goal and the level of their anxiety. Life-changing and life-enhancing goals are likely to be associated with greater anxiety than will be life-maintaining goals. Nevertheless, the pain from a hundred pin pricks can be worse than that caused by one stab wound.

In any service encounter the customer and the service provider are both engaged in self-presentation. The 'self' being projected in each case will to some extent not be the 'true' self. Many service providers are conditioned to present a professional self, which is far from their true self. Doctors, nurses, air crew, waitresses, and funeral undertakers are but a few examples of individuals who are expected to behave in a distinctive way when performing their role.

Likewise, customers may, by the nature of the service encounter, be expected to present themselves in a particular role. Patients are expected to let themselves be fully exposed, literally, if the service provider requires it. Borrowers are expected to reveal personal details of their financial situation and, sometimes, health, to qualify for a loan. Diners are expected to tip after a meal, air travellers are expected not to do so.

In essence the customer is presenting two selves – the service encounter self and the personal self. In both modes there will be anxieties. Anxieties for the service encounter mode will relate to the goal of the customer:

— 'Will I get the loan?'
— 'Will I arrive on time?'
— 'Will I enjoy the food?'
— 'Will I get a good night's sleep in this hotel?'
— 'Will I have any hassle returning this?'

Each of these service encounter anxieties can be anticipated in time by a service provider. More difficult to predict are the anxieties arising from the personal self mode of the customer. Fortunately, there has been sufficient psychological research on the causes of fear to enable us to categorise the major anxieties for which any service provider should be prepared:

— Fear of death
— Fear of physical injury and/or illness
— Fear of rejection
— Fear of going blank
— Fear of saying the wrong thing
— Fear of criticism
— Fear of exposing weaknesses
— Fear of failure
— Fear of loss of control.

Each of these fears can be reduced by action on the part of the service provider. Examples of such actions are given in Table 2.2.

As with the other arenas, there are five criteria which apply to psychic satisfaction:

(1) Customer expectations are established and in some way exceeded;
(2) The self-esteem of the customer is boosted by some action. (This could be as simple as using the customer's name);
(3) Customer goals are identified and the customer given an assessment of their feasibility;
(4) Service encounter anxieties are anticipated and reduced;
(5) General personal anxieties are anticipated and reduced.

Once again a rating of naught to five can be allocated to each criterion to measure the level of satisfaction. This approach is crude but can be a useful tool which any service company can use to get a measure of customer satisfaction by having the various criteria scored by a cross-section of service providers and customers (see Figure 2.3). If the scoring is done on an annual basis it will provide a useful indicator of customer satisfaction. In some cases, the findings will have the accuracy of the sundial rather than the atomic clock. For most companies, a reasonable idea of how they are measuring up to

Table 2.2   Coping with common anxieties of customers

Anxiety	Possible action by the services provider
Fear of death	Display safety instructions
	Encourage customer involvement in safety drills
	Display clearly emergency exits and ensure they are not blocked
	Seek out physical signs of anxiety and reassure individual displaying them
Fear of physical injury and/or illness	Be seen to inspect and take actions on possible hazards, e.g. broken glass
	Maintain high levels of cleanliness and personal hygiene
	Confront customers whose dress or behaviour is causing a nuisance to others
	In hotels provide name of local doctor
	Ensure appropriate clothing is worn by staff
	Adopt actions recommended for 'Fear of Death'
Fear of rejection	Practice drills for conveying 'bad news'
	Wherever possible offer alternatives
	Ensure customer is treated with dignity
	Provide privacy and time to reflect if decision likely to be a surprise
	Avoid building false hopes
	Underpromise and overdeliver
Fear of going blank	Listen
	Summarise situation to date
	Allow sufficient time for recall
	Do not pressurise

Fear of saying the wrong thing	Avoid jargon Regularly check understanding Provide reassurance Summarise discreetly using the 'right words'
Fear of criticism	Depersonalise criticism Give reasons for decision Be willing to accept/share at least some of the blame Try to end on a positive note
Fear of exposing weaknesses	Elicit only details you need to provide the service Use ego-boosting language Do not pressurise
Fear of failure	Elicit goals and expectations at an early stage Provide reassurance Offer alternatives Focus on positives
Fear of loss of control	Give regular information Provide reassurance Offer to inform others affected by any delay by customer Kill rumours fast

Please rate each of the criteria on a range of 0 to 5 as follows:

0 – Nowhere near
1 – Just beginning to get there
2 – Making some progress
3 – Making significant progress
4 – Almost there
5 – There

Product Satisfaction   **Rating**

- It performs (or will perform the function for which it has been purchased)
- Its performance is comparable to or exceeds that specified for products of similar price and availability
- It meets the physical needs of the customer in a manner which exceeds expectations
- Any deviations from performance standards will be dealt with in a manner which is acceptable to the customer at the time of purchase
- The product conforms fully to legal and regulatory requirements

Sub total:

Peripherals Satisfaction   **Rating**

- They add value to the core product
- They do not damage the health of the customer or induce the customer to so do
- They do not present the customer with ethical dilemmas
- They do not add to the cost of the purchase price of the core product
- They do not add to the inconveniencing of other customers

Sub total:

Ambience Satisfaction   **Rating**

- It adds value to the core product
- It is designed to put the customer at ease
- There is a synchronising of the physical design, furnishing and appearance of staff
- Layout, furnishings and such ancillary devices as lifts, escalators and mobile walkways
- Cleanliness, security and accessibility are clearly given special attention

Sub total:

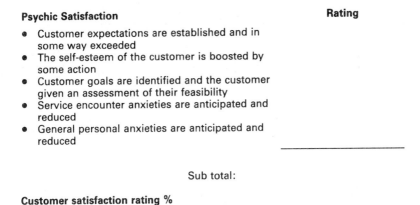

Psychic Satisfaction	Rating
• Customer expectations are established and in some way exceeded	
• The self-esteem of the customer is boosted by some action	
• Customer goals are identified and the customer given an assessment of their feasibility	
• Service encounter anxieties are anticipated and reduced	
• General personal anxieties are anticipated and reduced	
Sub total:	
Customer satisfaction rating %	

Figure 2.3 Customer satisfaction assessment

the needs and expectations of their customers is sufficient for them to decide where and how they need to do better.

2.7 CONCLUSION

Service industries across the world are growing in size and changing in nature. They account for an increasing proportion of the Gross National Product of developed countries; they are the battle ground of competitive advantage. Customers too are changing and this calls for new thinking.

Whereas in the Agricultural Revolution, commercial leadership went to those who knew how best to combine skill in adapting traditional farming methods with large-scale production, in the Industrial Revolution such leadership went to those who combined innovation and marketing with mass production. The Service Revolution is different; innovation, marketing and economies of scale still count, but competitive advantage is won or lost every day in a unique phenomenon – the service encounter where customer and service provider meet.

Although, like the stars, no two service encounters are the same, there are certain general principles which can guide us in studying how best to manage each encounter. The common link across diverse industries, different cultures, multifacet products, is customer care psychology.

By identifying the prevailing values and viewpoints of a society, the psychological make-up of individuals and the dominant mindset which each customer brings to a service encounter, we can determine how best to maximise customer satisfaction. This is no esoteric concept – it is the means of attracting and retaining those who provide service industries with the means to survival. Without an understanding of customer psychology, the service provider is working in the dark. No matter how alluring the advertisements, how attractive the product, how efficient the delivery system, in the final analysis it is how the customers are made to feel that determines their total satisfaction.

3 Customer Life-stages

3.1 INTRODUCTION

In customer care psychology 'social age' is as important as calendar age. It was only in the nineteenth century with the spread of industrialisation that this distinction began to take hold. The emergence of a middle class in the industrial societies of Britain, the United States and Western Europe brought into being formally organised schools for the young. This resulted in 'childhood' becoming a clearly definable life-stage.

As the twentieth century progressed, an increasing number of people stayed at higher educational institutes and so the social concept of 'adolescence' took shape. 'Youth' as a life-stage is a more recent phenomenon, defining a stage between the end of full-time secondary or tertiary education and the taking on of career or family commitments. This is the first customer life-stage of real significance.

'Middle age' is another social age of relatively recent significance. It is a reflection of the trend in Western Society to have fewer children per family and for the children to leave home in their early adulthood. As people live longer, the pressures on the middle aged are changing from responsibility for children to responsibility for elderly parents. This change has real significance for the use of customer psychology.

'Retirement' is the final social age though it can extend over decades of calendar age. The concept of retirement is associated with more leisure, less physical and intellectual prowess, social disengagement and increasing loneliness. Retirement is the one customer life-stage which is growing both in terms of numbers of people and numbers of years. In fact, as people retire earlier and live longer it is necessary to look at retirement as comprising the 'Young Old' and the 'Old Old'. Similarly, there is an argument for classifying young people as the 'Young Young' and the 'Old Young', but this could be confusing.

Therefore, in terms of analysing the psychology of customers at different life-stages we are dealing with seven 'stages':*

---

* Note the term 'life-stage' is used here to describe a socio-psychological period and does not refer to clinical psychology.

Childhood   0 – 15
Youth   15 – 20
Young adulthood 21 – 26
Mature adulthood 26 – 50
Middle age   50 – 65
Young old age   65 – 75
Old old age   75 onwards

Naturally, for any one individual these stages will not rigidly apply. Furthermore, developments in medicine, changes in social mores and in economics can blurr the boundaries. Nevertheless, the concept of customer life-stages enables us to identify those factors which can influence customers' perception of service quality as they progress through life.

3.2 CHILDHOOD

In terms of customer care psychology, childhood is a life-stage marked more by the influence which children can exert on customer choice rather than by their individual behaviour as buyers of goods and services.

Their influence has a marked effect on such industries as:

— Toys
— Records
— Films and videos
— Clothes
— Fast foods
— Sports equipment

The Swiss psychologist Jean Piaget put forward the theory that childhood consisted of a number of stages of learning, each of which had to be experienced in order for the child to develop its mental faculties such as memory, perceptual skills and other aspects of psychological growth. These theories are now questioned by other psychologists who have moved from the concept of broad developmental stages to one of examining different domains such as memory, problem-solving, and creativity. For example, they have found that memorising ability spurts forward from birth to age 5, then advances more slowly through middle childhood and adolescence.

One domain which is particularly important to service providers is that of social skills. Psychologists have found that acquiring these skills is partly a matter of learning that each social encounter has its distinctive mini-script. Take, for example, dining at a restaurant; very young children do not perceive dining out as a set of interactions by the various 'players'. By the age of 3 there is a growing awareness that different people play different roles; by 5 the mini-script is recognised in its component parts:

— Enter restaurant
— Sit at table
— Study menu
— Waitress writes order
— Waitress takes away menu
— Waitress brings food
— Eat food
— Waitress brings bill
— Leave table
— Pay money
— Leave restaurant

Children by the age of 5 not only become aware of scripts through personal experience, they also invent scripts with others on such service encounters as visiting the doctor, being in hospital, going on an aeroplane.

As they grow into adolescence, children develop the mini-scripts and devise subtle variations, as when eating at a fast food restaurant and at a hotel.

It is important for service providers to be aware of these mini-scripts and to build into them a role for the child which:

- Reduces or removes causes of anxiety, e.g. providing seating and cutlery which a child can handle. (This is becoming commonplace in restaurants but not in airline catering.)
- Enhances the self-esteem of the child without being patronising. (For example, speaking direct to a child who is capable of responding.)
- Provides a limited number of choices which are within the scope of a child's problem-solving abilities. (A child of say 7, offered a choice of five different styles of shoe is likely to be more confused than a child of 12.)

- Recognises the authority of the parent. The service provider should either stay neutral in influencing the behaviour of a child or be biased towards the parent. Supporting the child against the parent can have adverse consequences after the service encounter.

As children grow older they become more discerning as customers, but their perceptions will be shaped by their past experiences of how service quality reality matched their 'scripts'.

3.3   YOUTH

The years between 15 and 20 are a period of emotional ups and downs. About 40 per cent of the waking time of adolescents in the United States is spent on such leisure activities as:

— Meeting friends
— Watching TV
— Playing sports
— Following a hobby
— 'Thinking'

The remaining time is devoted to life-maintaining activities such as errands, eating, travelling, school and related work. Therefore, the two dominant mindsets in the customer psychology of the adolescent are 'short-term life enhancement' and 'short-term life maintenance'.

Research by the Chicago psychologist Mihaly Csikzentmihalyi suggests that American youth gets most satisfaction from meeting challenges that fit its developing skills and provide it with meaningful rewards. However, many take the path of least resistance and are prey to less stimulating activities such as watching TV and 'chatting'. These young people have not learned to make the connection between a challenge and feelings of personal fulfilment.

Prone to boredom, the adolescent can become preoccupied with:

(a) Parents who don't understand them;
(b) Break-ups in relations with the opposite sex;
(c) Worries about their personal appearance
(d) Worries about their popularity.

As they develop, adolescents become more proficient at dealing with life's 'downs'. They become more proficient at dealing with all types of encounters, particularly service encounters.

A survey of European youth over the period 1977 to 1987 by the McCann Erickson advertising agency summarised the development of consumption and its links with stages in the life-cycle.

Stage 1 from late childhood to early puberty is marked by:

(a) Reduction in the influence of parents and other authorities on buying decisions.
(b) Strong pressures from peer groups and the media to focus on buying brands – be they sweets or jeans.
(c) Expenditure devoted principally to consuming non-essentials.

Stage 2 from early teens until becoming one of the 'mature young' is marked by:

(a) Refinement of brand allegiances.
(b) Selection of products and brands which express individual identity.
(c) Recognition of influence of group pressure.
(e) Awareness of different demands on money available and the need to budget.
(f) Gradual development of a personal style.

The next stage phases into the mature young life-stage. Before considering this we shall examine other aspects of the psychology of young customers, since the adolescent phase is growing in importance socially, although declining in numbers throughout the 1990s. Therefore, the competition to capture the youth market in any service industry will intensify.

Youth is now a clearer customer life-stage than ever before. The youth market provides an early indication of the mature young and even active adult markets with which it overlaps. This is particularly true in such life-enhancing activities as entertainment, leisure wear, fast food restaurants and cosmetics.

Choices formed at an early customer life-stage can persist into later life, providing the choice is reinforced. This is one reason why banks have devoted enormous resources to attracting the 'youth market', despite it being unprofitable at early life-stages. The findings of a report by Euromoney and Garrick James Research (July 1990) provides evidence to support the view that banks have wasted their money in the quest for youth because they have ignored the importance of the service encounter in influencing customer psychology. The report revealed that although 80 per cent of young people interviewed had bank accounts, half said they would rather use a cash card than deal with a teller. Many were frightened of going into banks. This is due to:

• Social unease, particularly when the young earner is working class (as the majority would be).
• Fear of damaged self-esteem through rejection of a request or being made to feel ignorant.
• Concern about being persuaded to enter into a long-term commitment which would inhibit short-term gratification.

Youth in Western society is conditioned to consume; 'I buy therefore I am'. Want, not need, dominates the buying decision. Consumption has become an aid to self-expression and self-realisation.

Products are bought because they suit the youthful customer's life-style; so too are services. This can be seen particularly in such services as:

— Clothes retailing
— Hairdressing
— Pubs and clubs
— Travel
— Holiday arrangements

The McCann Erickson study identified six 'triggers' which are likely to influence those who are at the youth customer life-stage:

(1) The importance of style to convey that the user has sophistication – this must be conveyed in the audience's own idiom.
(2) The importance of achievement – suggesting that success is for the taking.
(3) The importance of fun and excitement.
(4) The importance of reassurance – but disguising it and ensuring it is not patronising.
(5) The importance of humour or wit.
(6) The importance of 'graphics' and different production values which are at the leading edge of technology.

The importance of 'dream' images on the youth psyche cannot be overemphasised in terms of creating an image of good service. 'Every age has its dreams and popular heroes, and in this respect the youth of today are no different. What is different, however, is the expression of those dreams . . . Each age needs its stories, its parables, its comic strips.' (McCann Erickson, *The New Generation*, 1989) The truth of this is to be seen in the popularity of such film heroes as Batman and Indiana Jones; in the growth of so-called 'adult' comics such as *Viz*; in the proliferation of film series like Rocky and Police Academy.

Service providers need to develop the ability to tune into the popular culture of youth, to identify what will attract the youth market without alienating those customers who are going through later life-stages. Ways in which this can be done include:

- Separation – providing 'youth' sections in department stores.
- Labelling – making clear to all customers that certain services are intended for specific life-stages.
- Mirroring – having service providers whose age, dress and behaviour accords with the youth life-stage.

Other forms of 'signalling', such as the choice and volume of music of the point of service delivery, can attract the targeted customer life-stage and repel others.

Bearing in mind that the primary focus of the youth customer life-stage is life enhancement, service providers should pay careful attention to the following attributes in any service encounter with youth:

- Service providers should either display a personal appearance and behaviour which is empathetic or be 'caring stereotypes'. Young customers want hairdressers, bar-tenders and clothes shop assistants who look like an idealised image of themselves and can communicate with them in their own idiom. They do not want such mirroring in encounters which for them are life maintaining, such as dealing with banks, hospitals or transport. Here the preference is for more stereotype dressing or uniforms, but with an empathetic manner which puts them at ease and reassures them that they are dealing with 'professionals'.
- Visual and audio stimuli are important in creating a sense of fun and excitement. They can also help to keep boredom at bay.
- Immediacy of gratification is important and calls for keen attention to stock levels, reduction of queues, giving early indications of delivery dates.
- The ability to differentiate between signs of boisterousness and

incipient violence; with clearly defined procedures for dealing with the latter.

As the boisterousness of youth gives way to embarking on a career and starting a family, the customer merges into the next life-stage – the young adult.

3.4   YOUNG ADULTHOOD

You realise you have entered the young adult customer life-stage when you and your parents go out to dinner and they let you pay the bill. Young adulthood is a time of changing relationships, a time of searching for roots, a time of setting and embarking on life goals. In terms of the customer care psychology model, it is above all a time of experiencing a series of life changes. These are likely to be associated with:

— Marriage
— Setting up home
— Arrival of first baby

In Western society there is a growing tendency to postpone the start of a family until a number of life-enhancing goals have been achieved. Furthermore, there is a marked increase in the existence of, and acceptance of, cohabitation rather than marriage. This can affect the providers of certain services such as mortgages and loans who have to deal with two separate customers rather than a married couple.

Until the mid-1980s the psychology of adulthood was greatly influenced by the theories of Erik Erikson. He and his colleagues at Yale put forward a hypothesis that as people approach each major period of adulthood, they pass through predictably unstable transitional periods, most marked around the age of 40 (the mid-life crisis).

More recent research casts doubt on this theory of predictable changes and suggests that it is changing times and different social values that affect how various 'cohorts' – groups of people born around the same time – move through life. Psychologist Bernice Neugarten of Northwestern University, USA developed the concept of the 'social clock' which guides our life. People who are 'out of sync' with the social clock will find life more stressful than those working to the same time.

A survey by *Time* magazine in July 1990 of young American adults provides an insight into an important social clock for those providing services in the coming decade.

> They have trouble making decisions. They would rather hike in the Himalayas than climb a corporate ladder. They have few heroes, no anthems, no style to call their own. They crave entertainment, but their attention span is as short as one zap of a TV dial. They hate yuppies, hippies and druggies. They postpone marriage because they fear divorce. They sneer at Range Rovers, Rolexes and red suspenders. What they hold dear is family life, local activism, US National Parks, penny loafers and mountain bikes.

The factors which are shaping the psyche of young adult customers in the USA are:

(1) A scepticism about marriage due to their experience as children of divorce.
(b) A rejection of materialism as a life goal and its replacement by a desire for job gratification.
(c) A recognition of the importance of higher education.
(d) A desire to travel and find oneself in the exotic East rather than search for ones cultural roots in Europe.
(e) A desire to give something back to society.

All these factors influence customer care psychology since they are producing a generation which is rootless and non-committal. Status symbols such as fast cars are perceived as carrying a social stigma. What the twenty-somethings seek is affordable quality. They want more for less. They seek authenticity in relationships. The day of 'Have a nice day' is over. Young adults seek added value, not only in terms of what they buy but in the situation where they buy it.

Their psyche has been injured sufficiently in life events to make them intolerant of any damage arising from a mishandled service encounter. Similar trends in the attitudes of young adults in Europe have been identified in a survey of business graduates reported in *International Management*, in July 1990.

Labelling them 'the Quality Generation', the survey revealed that these MBAs graduating from business schools in France, Italy,

Switzerland, Holland, Norway and Britain wanted 'quality time' with their families, quality work in their office, and quality in living.

Quality-of-life values such as social contribution, environmental protection and involvement in industries which create wealth, rather than make money, topped their list of life goals.

The important message for service providers in terms of young adult customers is to recognise that they have more choices when it comes not only to the substance of life-changing and life-enhancing decisions, but also to the nature of such decisions. Whereas previous generations had a choice as to where they would purchase a mortgage, arrange a wedding, have their children, the young adult of today can exercise the choice of either marrying or not marrying (yet living together); either setting up home or communing; either having a baby outside wedlock or not. Though these choices existed in the past they were not socially acceptable, now they are and the service provider must be prepared to meet these new life-styles and appeal to the changing values. An organisation which is seen to 'care' for its employees, customers and the environment will be the first choice of young adults in the 1990s.

3.5 MATURE ADULTHOOD

This customer life-stage covers what might be called the 'committed years'. During the period much of the expenditure of the adult is committed to such things as house purchase, education, family holidays, social obligations ranging from church support to membership of sports clubs.

This is a period of transitions, some of which overlap with the preceding and succeeding life-stages. There are, according to Professor Nancy K. Schlossberg of the University of Maryland, three types of transitions:

Anticipated transitions – the major life events we usually expect to be a part of adult life such as marrying, becoming a parent, starting a career, retiring.
Unanticipated transitions – the often disruptive events that occur unexpectedly, such as major surgery, a serious car accident, losing one's job, a surprise promotion, divorce, death of a loved one.
Non-event transitions – the expected events that do not occur, such

as not getting married, not having a baby, living longer than expected. (*Psychology Today*, May 1987)

Transitions are, in effect, 'life changes', many of which are bound to involve a need for service. Schlossberg suggests that how well individuals will cope with these life changes is determined by four factors:

(1) Situation
(2) Self
(3) Support
(4) Strategies

(1) *Situation* is determined by how the person perceives the life change. Is it positive, negative, welcome, unwelcome, expected or out of the blue? Does it come at the 'right time' or a 'bad time'? Is it surrounded by other stresses? Is it voluntary or enforced? Is it the beginning, middle or end of the life change? The service provider should seek out answers to these questions as early as possible in any service encounter. Naturally, the amount and nature of questioning will vary from one service provider (e.g. doctor) to another (e.g. banker).

(2) *Self* refers to the capacity of the individual to cope with the situation. What previous experience has the person had of similar situations? What options are available? How resilient is the person? How capable is he or she in dealing with ambiguity?

(3) *Supports* fall into two categories, financial and emotional. The former is easy to identify, the latter comes from family, friends and service providers. Dealing with life changes successfully requires that those close to us offer consistent support.

(4) *Strategies* are ways of coping with the impact of life changes. They can include ways of changing the situation, becoming more self-reliant, building up support, managing stress.

It is in our middle age that we are more likely to be faced with a series of life changes – children leaving home, parents becoming incapacitated, retirement, moving to a new home away from where we have lived during our working years are typical.

3.6 MIDDLE AGE

For the more affluent this customer life-stage is marked by an
increase in discretionary expenditure due to such factors as:

— End of paying for children's education;
— Inheritances from parents and older relatives who have died;
— Mortgages paid off;
— Life assurance policies matured.

A consequence of this is that customers in the middle-aged life-stage
are involved in an increasing number of life-enhancing service encounters – arranging holidays, refurbishing their homes, visiting their children in other countries, buying that 'something' they always wanted.

Life changes also come into play with greater speed as the mature
adult phase gives way to middle age, as previously outlined. Increasingly, people in this life-stage begin to plan for their retirement. This
can involve embarking on a second career, on a self-employed or
contract basis.

As customers, the middle aged become more demanding – they
have the economic capacity and increased self-assurance to demand
high standards of service quality. 'Life enhancement' implies that the
product or service being sought is not a necessity. The choices facing
the customer are: 'Shall we replace the car now or build a swimming
pool?' 'Shall we buy a caravan or tour the exotic East?' These are
very different from the choices of early years: 'Can we afford a car or
will I commute by train?' 'Can we afford a holiday or replace the
broken cooker?' As retirement approaches the middle aged move
into the next customer life-stage – the young old.

3.7 YOUNG OLD AGE

As our society gets older, the old are getting younger. We are having
to rethink what we mean by old age.

In most Western countries the proportion of people over 65 is
increasing. People over 65 will comprise 20 per cent of the population
of the United States by the year 2030; in Britain, the population aged
70 and over is expected to increase by 11 per cent between 1985 and
2000, compared with an increase of 18 per cent over the European
Community as a whole.

The number of people in Britain aged 80 and over (2 million in

1988) is now nearly 50 per cent greater than in 1961. According to the Government Statistical Service this age group is expected to increase to 2.9 million by the year 2025. It is this trend to longevity which makes it necessary to subdivide those over 60 into the young old and the old old.

The importance of the older customer is underlined in a survey in mid-1990 by the British market researchers Signal International. Entitled, *Over 55s. The Invisible Consumer*, the survey reveals that people in Britain over 55 account for £1 in every £3 spent by consumers. They spend because they want to, not to meet commitments. They do not have the debt burden of younger age groups as they own their houses outright. Many will see their disposable income increase through inheritance and improved private pension schemes.

Their functional age – the interplay of physical, psychological and social factors which influence their perceptions – is much younger than their chronological age. Research has revealed the need to distinguish between 'primary ageing' and 'secondary ageing'.

Primary ageing is a gradual process which results in deterioration in hearing and sight, a slowing of the reflexes, a lowering of stamina. This affects everyone, though the rate of primary ageing varies considerably.

Secondary ageing is to a large extent self-imposed. It is the result of abuse, disuse and disease. Too much alcohol, too little exercise, promiscuous behaviour, are all accelerators of secondary ageing. However, this is being held at bay as more and more older people take an increased interest in physical fitness.

Of particular interest in the study of customer psychology are the findings of Ed Diener, a University of Illinois psychologist. In a study of subjective well-being – happiness, life satisfaction, positive emotions – Diener reports: 'Most results show a slow rise in satisfaction with age . . . Young persons appear to experience higher levels of joy, but older persons tend to judge their lives in more positive ways.'

Daniel Ogilvie of Rutgers University has found that while money is often seen as a key to happiness, life satisfaction depends on how much time we spend doing things that are meaningful. Thus life-maintaining activities which are perceived as chores, result in low levels of customer satisfaction, particularly as we grow older. This can account for the view among service providers that 'old people are impatient'.

The motto of the young old age could be 'use it or lose it'. People fade away faster from disuse than they wear out from overuse. One great divide at this customer life-stage is that longevity is different for men and women. Women in Western societies tend to live seven or eight years longer than men. This means that services for the young old and, even more, for the old old need to be designed primarily to meet female needs. The more resources a woman has available (measured in education and income) the less likely she is to remarry. For men the trend is reversed.

Speaking at the celebration of Harvard University's three hundred and fiftieth anniversary in 1986, the political scientist Robert Binstock decried what he called 'the spectre of the aging society': 'the economic burdens of population aging; moral dilemmas posed by the allocation of health resources on the basis of age; labour market competition between older and younger workers within the context of age discrimination laws; seniority practices, rapid technological change; and a politics of conflict between age groups.' Binstock stated that these inaccurate perceptions reveal an underlying ageism, 'the attribution of these same characteristics and status to an artificially homogenised group labelled the "aged"'.

Woe betide the service provider who falls into this trap, failing to recognise that the needs and expectations of people over 65 cannot be lumped together. There is, however, a major distinction emerging in meeting the service needs of the young old and the old old. As people move into their eighties and nineties they inevitably become less mobile and there is often a deterioration in their mental faculties. A consequence of this is that service providers such as hairdressers, chiropodists, bankers and clothes retailers have to visit them. Therefore, service encounters take place in a different ambience and are often dominated by the 'carer' rather than the elderly customer.

3.8 OLD OLD AGE

In this final life-stage, the customer is often house-bound or in a residential home. Many suffer from disabilities and serious health problems. A significant number suffer serious injury from falls.

In due course, this age group will benefit from 'youth creep', the process of getting younger in capabilities and attitudes. Technology, particularly 'television shopping' will become an important means of purchasing goods and services.

Unfortunately, the old old age are the most vulnerable to exploitation and fraud. Therefore, service providers will need to review their service delivery practices carefully so that they are above suspicion. They must also be prepared to cope with false charges arising from the onset of memory loss and other mental deteriorations such as Alzheimer's disease.

Perhaps the most important thing that service providers should keep in mind about this customer life-stage is that in a caring society they will be judged by younger generations on how they are perceived to deal with the old old.

3.9 CONCLUSION

Strictly speaking, the term 'life-stages' is misleading, since it suggests a definitive series of clearly identifiable time-spans. In reality individual lives are more fluid; but for the purposes of developing a service quality strategy, life-stages is a useful concept. These changes need to be seen as steps in a fluid life-cycle as shown in Figure 3.1.

As we move along the cycle of life we face a variety of life changes, life enhancements and life-maintaining activities. The mix varies

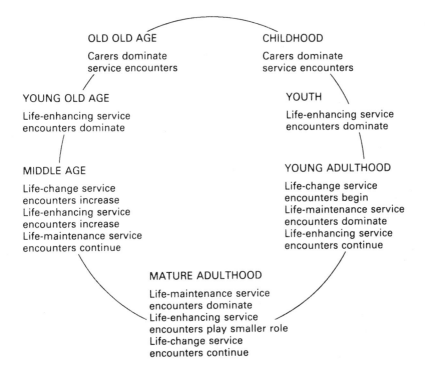

Figure 3.1 Customer life-cycle (idealised)

from person to person, from day to day and from year to year. Yet there is a certain symmetry as we pass from childhood to old old age.

In planning how best to satisfy their customer mix, a service provider needs to bear in mind the psychological factors which are likely to be working on the customer at different life-stages.

4 Influencing Customer Choice

4.1 INTRODUCTION

There are four options available to all customers:

(1) Purchase
(2) Rejection
(3) Postponement
(4) Substitution

Purchase decisions are of three types:

(1) Forced purchase due to the monopoly position of the service provider. Such decisions are sometimes tinged with resentment. The customer is predisposed to seek faults and complain in this situation.
(2) Reluctant purchase arises when the customer has a limited choice due to personal circumstances. For example, geographical factors may limit access to alternative service providers. Physical disabilities and/or economic constraints may require the customer to make do with 'second best'. Here too, customers are predisposed to seek faults, but may be reluctant to complain because they feel the fault is theirs. 'It's my own fault, I should have . . .'
(3) Ready purchase is the result of a product or service meeting or exceeding the needs and expectations of the customer in a situation of free choice. In this mode it is possible that dissatisfaction will be as much the failure to live up to expectations as any tangible fault.

Reject decisions are of four types:

(1) Price of the product/service is more than the customer can afford.
(2) The product or service on offer does not meet the needs or expectations of the customer.

(3) The manner of the service provider adversely determined or influenced the purchase decision.

(4) Perceptions of the service provider or previous bad experience has a negative impact on the purchase decision.

Postponement may be short term, medium term or long term. Whatever the time-span involved the service provider has an opportunity to reduce it by repackaging or gaining purhase commitment. Repackaging may take the form of unbundling the product or service – 'Buy the table now and the chairs later'; 'Take out this limited insurance policy now and the rest later.'

Gaining purchase commitment can be achieved through:

— Accepting a deposit;
— Prepurchase instalment payments;
— Initiating a rental or leasing agreement which can be changed to outright purchase at a later date.

Substitution comes in many guises. It is the result of trade-offs by the customer. Such trade-offs *vis-à-vis* the desired product or service may be in terms of:

• Restricted functions
• Reduced reliability
• More limited guarantees
• Restricted choice
• Less attractive appearance
• Greater effort required of customer
• Less after-sales service.

Restricted functions may refer to a product or a service. A food processor with three attachments may be the substitute of one with five. An insurance policy covering loss up to a limit of £5000 may be the substitute for one of a higher limit.

The factors which influence customer choice are varied. Table 4.1 outlines a number of both physical and psychological needs of customers in terms of such services as:

(a) Airlines
(b) Hotels
(c) Restaurants

(d) Department stores
(e) Cinemas
(f) Car hire
(g) Pubs
(h) Petrol stations
(i) Hairdressers
(j) Estate agents

In many cases, these service providers concentrate on satisfying physical needs and pay little attention to the psychological ones. However, it is in terms of both types of needs that judgement of customer satisfaction is made.

4.2 PSYCHIC ADDED-VALUE

A major aim of any manufacturer or service provider should be to optimise psychic added-value and minimise psychic damage. Psychic added-value is the boost which a customer experiences when using a product or a service. It augments or damages the tangible factors influencing customer perception. Table 4.2 gives examples of standard satisfiers, satisfier boosters and dissatisfiers. Standard satisfiers meet the expectations of customers. They do not provide psychic added-value; at best they will have a neutral effect on customer satisfaction. Satisfier boosters do provide added-value, no matter how small, by exceeding customer expectations they enhance satisfaction and provide a sense of customer care. Dissatisfiers reduce the satisfaction level of customers leaving them discontent and with a sense of annoyance which can rapidly move to a perceptions of victimisation as shown in Table 4.3.
     Sources of psychic added-value are:

- Enhanced self-esteem   – Customer made to feel important in the eyes of the service provider.

- Reduced anxiety   – Fears and concerns, identified, articulated and assuaged by behaviour of service provider.

- Increased
  self-confidence   – Customer made to feel proficient in use of equipment; knowledgeable in

64

Table 4.1 Physical and psychological needs of customers

Service industry	Physical needs	Psychological needs
Airlines	Fast transportation Feeding Safety	Security Reliability Diversion or peace on flight Respect of concerns Information
Hotels	Accommodation Feeding Safety Comfort	Security Recognition Member of 'the club' Lack of hassle Reinforce positive self-image
Restaurants	Feeding Comfort	Reassurance Put at ease Recognition Appropriate pacing
Department store	Goods No hassle refunds	Effective guidance Reliability Discreet attention Knowledgeable advice
Cinema	See film	Entertainment Comfort Uninterrupted viewing Security

Service	Core benefit	Attributes
Car hire	Transportation by car	Availability Reliability Security Support of positive self-image No hassle procedures
Pub	Drink Food	Congenial company Recognition Security
Petrol station	Fuel for car	Speed of service Safety Reliability
Hairdresser	Cut and/or shaping of hair Manicure/pedicure Shaving	Support for positive self-image
Estate agent	Help purchase or sell accomodation	Reliability Communication Reassurance

Table 4.2   Standard satisfiers, satisfier boosters and dissatisfiers

	Standard satisfiers	*Satisfier boosters*	*Dissatisfiers*
TANGIBLE	Competitively priced	Price significantly less than competitors	Price higher than competitors
	Meets performance specification	Exceeds performance specification	Fails to meet performance specification
	Limited numbers produced	Exclusive	More prevalent than expected
	Lasts as long as expected	Lasts longer than expected	Does not last as long as expected
	Failures put right without hassle	No failure	Hassle involved in putting failures right
PSYCHIC	Neutral effect on self-esteem	Enhance self-esteem	Damages self-esteem
	Neutral effect on self-confidence	Enhances self-confidence	Damages self-confidence
	Neutral effect on social status	Enhances social status	Reduces social status
	No significant memories/feelings evoked by product/service	Good memories/feelings evoked	Bad memories/feelings evoked
	A good experience	An unexpectedly good experience	A bad experience

understanding of advice or service offered by service provider.

- Comfort   – Customer made to feel physically and mentally at ease by caring ambience and behaviour of service provider.

- Social status – Customer made to believe that product/service will enhance social status.

- Reassurance   – Customer convinced that decision to purchase goods or service is the right one.

In customer care psychology it is necessary to reinforce these factors and take action to avoid such sources of psychic damage as:

Table 4.3 Preventing annoyance becoming victimisation

Cause of annoyance	Cause of victimisation	Preventions
Aircraft delay (business)	Late for meeting	Offer to contact meeting organiser and explain reason for delay
Aircraft delay (pleasure)	Missing holiday time	Offer diversion (coach trip); voucher for drink, books, magazines. Provide 'holiday extra' such as bottle of sparkling wine with meal.
Equipment breakdown	Unable to do vital job	Offer temporary replacement Provide alternative at low cost (e.g. visit to laundrette while washing machine broken).
Hotel room not ready	Unable to change clothes, freshen up, etc. Unable to start holiday	Offer temporary accommodation Offer diversion such as 'free ticket' to cinema, theatre.
Food on menu not available	Unable to enjoy your 'favourite thing'.	Offer free starter or dessert or drink
Item out of stock at supermarket	Wasted time and money on journey	Offer alternative at a small discount. Offer to hold item for next visit or to deliver it to customer.
Shop unexpectedly closed	Wasted time and money on journey	Place apology and brief details of cause of closure in prominent position. Give time of reopening and/or alternative suppliers.

- Reduced self-esteem   – Customer made to feel that product/service is 'too good for the likes of him/her' by service provider; or is ignored.

- Heightened anxiety   – Customers fears and worries increased by behaviour of service provider.

- Reduced confidence   – Customer made to feel clumsy in use of equipment or in seeking a service.

- Discomfort   – Customer made uncomfortable by ambience and/or manner of service provider.

- Reduced social status   – Customer made to feel that he/she is getting 'second-class service'.

- Lack of assurance   – Customer not helped in reaching a purchase decision or given 'standard treatment'.

4.3   SHAPING CUSTOMERS' PSYCHOLOGY

There are ten major factors which influence customers' perceptions. Alphabetically, they are:

(1) Accessibility
(2) Communications
(3) Competence
(4) Courtesy
(5) Credibility
(6) Reliability
(7) Responsiveness
(8) Security
(9) Tangibles
(10) Understanding

The relative influence of each factor will, of course, vary from one individual to another and from situation to situation. However, there is a host of indicators which service providers can use to make a positive impact on customer perceptions (see Table 4.4).

Table 4.4 Major influences on customer care psychology*

Influencer	Impact on customer perceptions	Indicators
Accessibility	Signifies respect for individual's need	Availability of staff Time taken to contact 'the right person' Clear signs Answer machines Emergency contacts
Communications	Heightens awareness of situation and creates realistic expectations	Use of plain words Telephone service Clear instructions Straightforward letters Active listening Treated as an intelligent individual Forewarning of changes
Competence	Conveys professionalism and gives reassurance	Right first time Comprehensive knowledge Sound advice Mastery of procedures Ability to deal with 'one-off' situations Smooth rhythm of service
Courtesy	Establishes rapport and puts at ease	Use of pleasantries at beginning and end of encounter Friendly behaviour

continued on p. 70

Table 4.4 continued

Influencer	Impact on customer perceptions	Indicators
		Caring attitude
		Respect for individual
		Active listening
		Use name of customer
		Use name of self
		Appropriate pacing
		Dress and other aspects of personal appearance
		Manner of speaking
		Explanation of any delays in service
		Handling complaints
		Handling compliments
		Providing choices
		Acknowledgement of customers' concerns, needs and expectations
Credibility	Confirms that customer has made right choice and that service promises will be kept	Product knowledge
		Procedures knowledge
		Keeping promises
		Admitting mistakes
		Consistency in decisions
		Consistency in provision of services/products
		Consistency in answers

Reliability	Develops trust	Accuracy of data supplied Value of advice Swift return of messages and telephone calls Time-keeping Meeting promised deadlines Consistently high standards Keeping promises
Responsiveness	Reinforces self-esteem	Follow up on queries Speed of reactions Anticipation of needs Provision of back-up resources Awareness of customers' time pressures and working within them Warning of delays
Security	Provides physical and psychological comfort	Confidentiality Rigorous enactment of security checks and controls Professional conduct Reassurance regarding fears and concerns Privacy

continued on p. 72

Table 4.4 continued

Influencer	Impact on customer perceptions	Indicators
Tangibles	Influences perceptions and choices	Appearance of staff Appearance of premises Quality of documents Provision of aids to comfort Clear signage and layout Quality of furniture and equipment
Understanding	Cements relationships	Flexibility Expressions of genuine sympathy Willingness to do something extra Exhibition of the 'human touch' Empathising Pacing appropriate to customers' needs

* Assuming prices of competing services are the same or similar.

4.4 SERVICE ENCOUNTERS

Judgement of the various indicators is made by customers every time they come in contact with the provider of a service. This we referred to as the 'service encounter' in Chapter 2. We shall now analyse the concept in greater detail. Customer care psychology in terms of service encounters depends on the *nature* and *function* of the encounter.

Nature of encounter may be:

- Isolated – service provider is not present in any way at point of delivery (e.g. cash dispensers).
- Sightless – service provider and customer are in blind contact (e.g. on telephone).
- Face to face – both service provider and customer are in visible contact.

Function of encounter may be:

- Awareness – customer is consciously and subconsciously aware of type and standard of service (e.g. arriving unaccompanied into a hotel room).
- Retrieval – customer is seeking action by service provider in putting right a deviation from promised/expected service (e.g. lost luggage at airport).
- Dependency – customer has high dependency on service provider to satisfy a need which calls for scare expertise (e.g. legal advice).
- Optional – customer is seeking to satisfy a need for which there are many alternative service providers (e.g. grocery shopping).
- Transforming – customer is seeking satisfaction of a need which will result in a significant change to the customer (e.g. buying a house).
- Facilitating – customer is seeking satisfaction of a need which will make life easier/more pleasant (e.g. booking a holiday).
- Impulse – customer is seeking instant gratification of an unplanned need, stimulated by advertising or other influence at a point in time (e.g. buying an ice-cream).
- Chore – customer is under some degree of pressure to satisfy an externally sourced need (e.g. paying a parking fine, cashing a cheque).

Table 4.5 Expressions of feelings describing service encounters

Negative feelings	Positive feelings
I was made to feel a fool (Bank customer)	I was made to feel no effort was too much (Bank customer)
We were treated like cattle (Airline customer)	We were treated like royalty (Airline customer)
I felt like a freak (Clothes shop customer)	I felt like a bride (Clothes shop customer)
I felt I was a nuisance (Hotel customer)	I felt at home (Hotel customer)
I felt rushed (Restaurant customer)	I felt spoiled (Restaurant customer)
I felt I must be invisible (Shop customer)	I felt welcomed (Shop customer)
I felt angry at how I was treated (Telephone company customer)	I was made to feel I'd done the right thing (Telephone company customer)
I felt ignored (Hairdresser customer)	I felt they really cared (Hairdresser customer)
I felt I never wanted to see them again (Holiday hotel customer)	I feel I want to go back next year (Holiday hotel customer)
I felt embarrassed (Hospital patient)	I felt they were on my side (Hospital patient)

The function of an encounter is closely associated with the dominant mind-sets of life-change, life enhancement and life maintenance discussed in Chapter 2.

Whatever the nature or function of an encounter it is necessary to manage it in a manner which conveys a genuine sense of customer care. It is important to remember that a service encounter is always 'managed'. If the service provider is managing it, the opportunity exists to provide customer care. When the customer has to manage it (e.g. attracting attention, following up on promises) customer care is absent. Table 4.5 gives typical examples of how customers convey their feelings about service encounters. Ways of recovering a poor service encounter are outlined in Table 4.6.

Table 4.6 How to recover a poor customer care situation

Listen	– Let customers get complaints off their chests, but do not tolerate personal abuse or bad language.
Apologise	– Even if you are not at fault personally, apologise on behalf of the organisation.
Remedy	– Take or promise some action to remedy the situation – use 'action words' such as 'I'll phone/contact/see so and so now/today/by such a time.'
Empathise	– Show you understand how customer feels; why complaint appears justified.
Redress symbolically	– Provide some token, cup of tea, voucher, pen, flowers, use of 'private office', bathroom to help make amends.
Follow-up	– Check that promises made have been kept.

Avoidance is always preferable to recovery; if the service provider is to manage any encounter effectively it will be necessary to acquire a range of customer care skills.

4.5 CUSTOMER CARE SKILLS

There are seven clusters of customer care skills:

(1) *Seeking* – behaviours which politely convey to the customer a need for a response.
(2) *Defining* – behaviours which indicate in objective terms a course of action to meet the needs/expectations of the customer.
(3) *Expressing* – behaviours which indicate reactions evoked by the statements of a customer.
(4) *Supporting* – behaviours which help to enhance the positive feelings and/or reduce the negative feelings of the customer.
(5) *Bridging* – behaviours which link different parts of an interaction with the customer.
(6) *Pacing* – behaviours which control the rate at which other behaviours are being brought into play in an interaction with the customer.
(7) *Spacial* – behaviours which define spacial relationships with the customer and provide a relationship context in which the customer experiences the other behaviours.

Details of each cluster are given in Table 4.7.

Used properly these behaviours will influence positively the sense of customer care, since they are felt in the subconscious as well as in the conscious mind of customers. Used wrongly they greatly reduce any feelings of customer care. How to select the appropriate customer care skill in different situations is shown in Table 4.8.

4.6 CUSTOMER PSYCHOLOGY CHAINS

Chains are interrelated patterns of behaviour triggered by a customer's service experience.

The basic model of a positive chain (which may be the outcome of one or a number of effective service encounters) is:

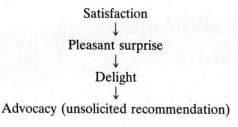

The basic model of a negative chain is:

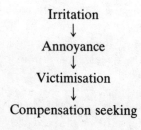

Other chains:

- Communication chain:

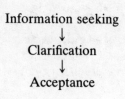

continued on p. 85

Table 4.7 Customer care skills

Behaviour cluster	Typical behaviours	Verbal indicators
Seeking: behaviours which reveal a need for a complementary response by the customer.	*Seeking information*: indicates that data is required before servicing can be provided.	'Please tell me what happened.'
	Seeking clarification: indicates that uncertainty exists about content of communication from customer.	'Can you please repeat that?'
	Seeking confirmation: indicates that uncertainty exists about interpretation of communication from customer.	'Let me see if I've got this right.'
	Seeking agreement: elicits support for proposed course of action.	'Would it be acceptable to you if we . . .'
Defining: behaviours which indicate in objective terms a course of action to meet the needs/expectations of the customer.	*Proposing specifics*: defining precise action to be taken within a specified time.	'What we'll do is this.'
	Proposing alternatives: defining options which can be chosen by the customer.	'What we can do is either . . . or if you prefer . . .'
	Confirming: defining agreed course of action.	'What we've agreed therefore is . . .'
	Giving information: providing facts in response to questions.	'The first flight is at . . .'

continued on p. 78

Table 4.7 continued

Behaviour cluster	Typical behaviours	Verbal indicators
Expressing: behaviours which indicate objective reaction evoked by the statements of the customer.	Giving advice: providing opinions in response to questions.	'The best thing to do is . . .'
	Agreeing: expressing accord with the customer's statements.	'I agree.'
	Disagreeing: rejecting the validity of the customer's statements.	'I'm sorry, but that's not how we see it.'
	Interrupting: indicating frustration with the behaviour of the customer.	'Could you just hold on a second?'
Supporting: behaviours which help to enhance the positive feelings and/or reduce the negative feelings of the customer.	Sympathising: expressing regret at situation.	'I'm sorry to hear that.'
	Empathising: expressing a shared understanding of the situation.	'I can see how you must have felt.'
	Apologising: accepting responsibility for the situation.	'Sorry, it's our fault.'
	Reassuring: confirming the correctness of customer's actions.	'You did the right thing in bringing this to our attention.'
	Allaying fears: reducing anxiety about consequences of future action.	'There's nothing to worry about. It will go like clockwork.'
	Enhancing: strengthening confidence of customer.	'You've made the right choice, I'm sure.'
	Calming: reducing irritation/anger caused by past events.	'What a nuisance. Let me try to put it right straightaway.'

Bridging: behaviours which link different parts of an interaction.	*Pleasantries*: indicating by use of conventional phrases the beginning or end of an interaction	'Good morning' 'Good bye'
	Greeting: using name of customer to indicate degree of intimacy sought in the interaction.	'Mrs Jones . . .' 'Betty . . .'
	Building: using information from another behaviour to achieve objective.	'In addition to . . . would you be interested in . . .'
	Summarising: restating in a shorter form the outcomes of previous behaviours.	'So, in effect your complaint is . . .'
Pacing: behaviours which control the rate at which other behaviours are being brought into play in an interaction.	*Acknowledging*: indicating awareness of the presence of the customer.	(Usually non-verbal: smile or wave.)
	Prioritising: indicating time when service will be provided.	'I'll be with you shortly.' 'I'll just have to . . .'
	Accelerating: indicating that speed of service will be relatively rapid.	(Usually shown in speed of talk and other action, rather than content, but can be verbal.) 'OK but I'll have to be quick.'

continued on p. 80

Table 4.7 continued

Behaviour cluster	Typical behaviours	Verbal indicators
	Decelerating: indicating that speed of service will/can be slower.	'Now, don't rush, we've plenty of time.' 'Would you like a break before the next course?'
	Monitoring: controlling the speed of the transaction.	'Before we deal with that could you . . .'
	Standing	
	Sitting	
	Sending	'Please go to . . .'
	Leaving	'Please wait there – I'll be back shortly.'
	Isolating	'Please stand/sit other there.'
Spacing: behaviours which define spatial relationship with customer and provide a location context in which the customer experiences the other behaviours.	Accompanying	'Mr Smith will take you to . . .'

Table 4.8 How to select the appropriate customer care skill

Situation: Dealing with complaints made in person

Action	Behaviour
Show concern	
Be seen to give the customer the benefit of the doubt in stating complaint even when it is not our fault.	Bridging Supporting Seeking
Provide privacy either in terms of space or time.	Pace Space
Take prompt action Do not keep customer waiting without forewarning of likely period of waiting and checking agreement to wait.	Define Seek
Listen Avoid interrupting. Let customer fully voice complaint before making any response.	Pace

continued on p. 82

Table 4.8 *continued*

Situation: Dealing with complaints made in person	
Action	*Behaviour*
Ask questions but avoid interrogating.	Seek
Give customer time to answer.	Express
Do not seek to apportion blame.	Pace
Manage your reaction	Express
Avoid:	Define
– taking the complaint personally.	Pace
– anticipating outcome before customer has finished.	
– 'switching off'.	
– becoming defensive.	
– making excuses.	
– blaming 'them' or another part of 'the organisation'.	
Referring to another official	Define
Keep customer in the picture.	Support
Explain reason for referring elsewhere.	Bridge
Introduce customer and brief your colleague.	
Seek remedy	Seek
Agree course of action, specify what will happen and when.	Define
Find a solution which is most acceptable to our company	
and our customer.	
Provide remedy	Define
Make sure the agreed action is carried out before the	Seek
customer does.	

Situation: Complaints made by telephone	
Action	*Behaviour*
Act similarly to complaints made in person. In addition:	
Sound concerned (People tend to be more aggressive when phoning complaints.)	Support
Make notes of complaint, plus name and telephone number of the customer.	Seek
Apologise for the inconvenience of having to telephone. Offer to phone back.	Support Define
If call has to be transferred explain reason to customer and brief colleague.	Define
Avoid asking customer to telephone back unless this is preferred by customer.	Define Support

continued on p. 84

Table 4.8 continued

Situation: Complaints made by letter	
Action	*Behaviour*
Letter to be seen by one of the management team	
Reply same day – at least send acknowledgement saying what will be done and when.	Support Define Express
Adapt standard reply where appropriate.	
Have any 'difficult' reply checked (and signed) by manager or deputy.	
Remember, whether the complaint is made in person, by telephone or by letter, seek to show customers care, concern, courtesy, reassurance and flexibility by your behaviour.	

- Miscommunication chain:

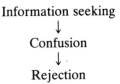

Information seeking
↓
Confusion
↓
Rejection

- Trust chain:

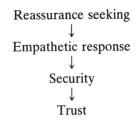

Reassurance seeking
↓
Empathetic response
↓
Security
↓
Trust

- Mistrust chain:

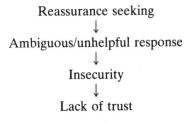

Reassurance seeking
↓
Ambiguous/unhelpful response
↓
Insecurity
↓
Lack of trust

- Pleasure chain:

Comfort
↓
Luxury
↓
Indulgence

- Pain chain:

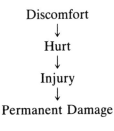

Discomfort
↓
Hurt
↓
Injury
↓
Permanent Damage

By using the appropriate customer care skills it is possible to reinforce positive chains and break negative chains.

These psychological chains are influenced not only by behaviour but by environmental factors, particularly colour and music.

4.7 THE COLOUR OF CUSTOMER CARE

Colour is reflected light. Our brain responds to the energy source which emanates from each colour. Different colours have different effects on people, but there has been sufficient research to show that some colours have similar effects on the majority of people (see Table 4.9). Just as sound produces vibrations which affect our hearing and enable us to interpret different sounds and form them into patterns, colour has a similar effect on sight. As energy waves, colour, like sound, creates in us perceptions of intensity, hue and shade, and loudness, pitch and tone in the case of sound.

Service providers can use colour to stimulate desired reactions by their customers; often, the adverse effects of colour are ignored or there is a lack of awareness that certain colours and colour combinations can stimulate negative perceptions. In the 1970s, the American airline Braniff distinguished itself from competitors by having the exterior of its aircraft painted in pastel colours. This was based on the whim of Mrs Braniff and not on customer desire. The initial novelty soon wore off and airline customers showed their preference for 'technology based' colours, such as different shades of silver and blue, rather than 'boudoir' colours. Braniff Airlines is no more.

Colour is a favourite device for 'branding' a service. Banks, retail chains, fast food chains, and oil companies all sport corporate colours. This can give a sense of security or reassurance to the customer, particularly when away from home base. One danger is that less scrupulous competitors will copy a distinctive colour scheme and 'house style' of a company name, in the hope of deceiving customers and supplying them with lower quality goods and service. This calls for eternal vigilance on the part of the original service provider. Harrods of London have fought court cases across the world to safeguard the integrity of their distinctive colour and title lettering.

Colour can reflect changes in social values and viewpoints. A survey in mid-1990 by Du Pont, makers of carpet fibres, found that carpet buyers in the United States were turning to blue 'to reflect the swing from the materialistic 1980s towards the caring 1990s'. Plotting earlier changes in colour preference, research in the United States pinpoints a marked preference for reds in times of war with a move to light blues, greys, black and browns in times of economic stress.

4.8 COLOUR SUPPORT FOR SERVICES AND PRODUCTS

Colour can be used to make a positive impact on customers in creating the best ambience for service encounters. In her book *The Language of Colours*, Dorothee L. Mella, a 'colour psychologist', suggests the ways in which colour imagery can be used in decor. I have adapted her suggestions in Table 4.9, integrating them with my own findings.

There is evidence to suggest that colour preferences change with the age of a customer. Younger customers in retail settings respond well to the stimulation of high energy colours such as bright reds, oranges and yellows. Older customers in their seventies and eighties prefer warm colours such as pink and peach.

There is a growing use of yellows, beige and neutral light colours in hotels as these reinforce feelings of comfort and security.

4.9 OTHER USES OF COLOUR

In his book *Manwatching*, Desmond Morris comments on our reluctance to eat blue foods and drink blue drinks. This he claims is a throwback to the eating habits of our primeval ancestors whose natural foods were nuts and seeds (brown and yellow), fruits and roots (orange, red and white) and leaves and shoots (green). Whatever its origins, the bias against blue as a colour of food is but one example of in-built colour preferences and prejudices. Colour is therefore an important tool in creating brand images and maintaining customer loyalty. The pale green of Heinz Beans tins, the red of Coca-Cola cans, Johnny Walker Black Label (or the cheaper Red Label) are instantly recognisable by customers; so much so that less scrupulous competitors copy them in the often justified expectation that customers 'buy the colour' without reading the contents.

The colour of precious metals is used to impart a sense of luxury in the quality of an intangible service. 'Gold' credit cards are supplanted by 'platinum' credit cards. Silver, gold and platinum are used to describe standards of airline service, hotel suites, holiday tours and funeral services.

Table 4.9 The use of colour in service encounters

Colour	Effects	Types of services best suited to colour	Comments
Red	Creates a strong physical image	Sports centres, dance halls, restaurants	Red has to be combined with other colours, such as black, where customers are expected to linger.
Orange	Creates high energy image	Speedy services such as fastfood, repairs while you wait	Best used when a high through-put of customers is required.
Yellow	Communicates need for attention	Communications and entertainments industries	Useful for encouraging impulse buying.
Green	Health and environmental awareness	Whole-food restaurants, environmental support services such as garbage collection, food retail chains	Has positive image if colour has been traditional (e.g. Lloyds Bank) but can have negative impact if perceived by customers as 'jumping on the band wagon'.

Light blue	Projects a creative image.	Technology based services such as computer maintenance, quick printing.	Can create a sense of calm.
Gold	Creates an image of security and wealth.	Bankers, jewellers, up-market services.	Can put off less affluent customers. Unless skilfully used it can appear garish.
Grey	Passive image, anonymous and clinical but also technical.	Repair services, stations and airports.	Needs blending with other colours to marry warmth with technical efficiency.
Pink	Conveys a caring, feminine image.	Fashion stores, children's crèches, perfume departments.	Needs to avoid looking too sugary or can alienate male customers and some females.
Black	Authority and bereavement image.	Funeral parlours, high-level consultancy services with an emphasis on confidentiality.	Can be off-putting unless blended with other colours.

From cradle (pink for a girl, blue for a boy) to grave, colour is used to position products and services.

4.10 CONCLUSION

Customer choice and subsequent satisfaction are influenced by a range of both tangible and intangible factors.

The ability to identify the full range of such factors and to select the appropriate skills determines competitive advantage. At the centre of customer care is the service encounter. Once satisfied on price and on the tangible quality of the product or service purchased, the customer seeks psychic added-value. It is in the mind of the customer as much as in the market-place that customer care leadership is won.

5 Managing Customer Care

5.1 INTRODUCTION

Customer care – good or bad – is no accident, but is the outcome of a company's service quality system. All organisations have such a system. For some it is an informal, unstructured system which provides low levels of service; for others it is a well thought out, effectively structured system which delivers consistently high levels of service. The irony is that it takes no more effort to devise a well-structured system than it does to cope with an unstructured one. This section describes the components that combine together to provide the type of service quality system which will maximise profit and stimulate growth by providing customer satisfaction. Subsequent sections will deal with each component in depth, drawing on practical experience.

Customer care is the outcome of meeting a customer's service needs and expectations.

— Failure to meet needs or expectations = poor customer care
— Meeting needs and expectations = adequate customer care
— Meeting needs and exceeding expectations = good customer care

The ability to meet customer needs consistently in a manner that exceeds expectations will not in itself result in a customer care differentiation. For that, it is necessary to meet needs and exceed expectations in a manner that consistently outmatches the competition.

Customer care is therefore a key to profitability through competitive advantage. It is both a business philosophy and a business practice, calling for a melding of strategies, values, behaviour, systems, and structures. Figure 5.1 shows the interaction of the main components of any service quality system. Using the model as a map we shall start at the top, making a quick tour of all the components. Subsequently, we shall be revisiting them at greater length.

5.2 MISSION

The start of any service quality system should be a clear statement of why the company exists – a mission statement. Such a statement

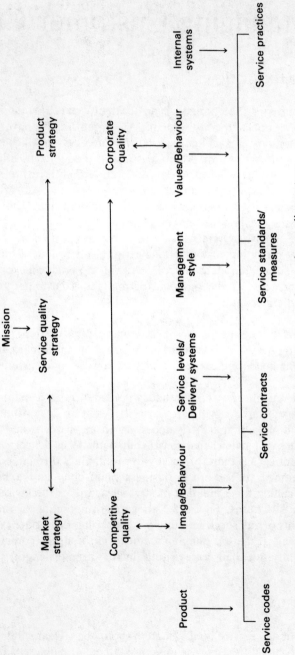

Figure 5.1 The main components of a service quality system

should be pithy, unambiguous and should set the tone for all company activities, particularly its service quality.

Any mission statement should emanate from the chief executive. In drawing up the statement there should be full consultation with managers who eventually have to be seen to believe in it and live by it.

5.3 STRATEGIES

From the mission statement which provides an enduring set of guiding principles will emerge some strategies with various time frames:

- The marketing strategy defines those customer segments which the company seeks to serve.
- The product strategy specifies the type and range of product (or service) which the company will provide for each customer segment.
- The service quality strategy outlines the manner in which the product (or service) will de delivered to each customer segment.

Any service quality strategy has to provide for two related strands:

(1) Competitive quality
(2) Corporate quality

5.4 COMPETITIVE QUALITY

Competitive quality has an external focus on the market-place. It is that part of the service quality system which influences the perceptions of customers; influencing their choice of one company in preference to another. Competitive quality is the most visible part of the system since it comes into play at every point of contact with the customer, be it face to face, by letter or telephone.

There are a number of components which shape and are shaped by competitive quality:

- Product (or service)
- Image

- Customer contact behaviour
- Service levels
- Delivery systems

Customers come to an organisation to find a product (or service) which will satisfy a need. The characteristics of the product, particularly its price, has a marked impact on customers' perceptions of competitive quality. When there is little to choose between products, other factors influence customer choice.

The image of the company influences both the perceptions and expectations of the customer. Many things combine to create an image – advertising, word-of-mouth reputation, personal experience. Some companies have developed an image of providing high levels of service quality. Failure to meet or exceed the resultant expectations will dent its image. Similarly, as we have seen in earlier chapters, a company with a poor service quality image can change this by exceeding expectations. In the end, our image of a company is determined by our experience of it – how its employees behaved towards us.

Behaviour has a pivotal role to play in any service quality system. People can choose their behaviour to project a good or bad image. The behaviour which manifests itself in competitive quality is influenced by many of the factors which determine corporate quality. Indeed, competitive and corporate quality are the unseparated Siamese twins of any service quality system; they prosper or die together.

The types of behaviour most appropriate in competitive quality situations can be defined and developed in a manner which will result in a distinctive style of service. Such a style should be clearly perceived by customers regardless of what level of service they are buying.

All service has to be paid for. Some organisations, such as airlines, provide various service levels. Others, such as de-luxe cruisers offer only one level. Whatever the number of levels, it is necessary to define the differentiating factors which will determine the competitive quality of each level. If your company's 'standard service' is on a par with your competitor's more expensive 'super service', you have a clear competitive advantage.

The service level(s) will in turn determine the service delivery systems for each customer segment. Delivery systems range from hotel reception to cabin service; from telephone calls to self-service petrol pumps; from cash dispensers to supersonic transport. Whatever the type of service and the level, every service quality system has to determine the most customer friendly service delivery systems which it can provide at the price which customers are willing to pay.

As with other facets of competitive quality, service delivery systems are influenced not only by customer needs and expectations, but by corporate quality.

5.5   CORPORATE QUALITY

In contrast to its twin, corporate quality has an internal focus. Whereas competitive quality determines the service quality differentiation of a company, corporate quality determines its service quality ethos. It shapes the perceptions of employees, shareholders, regulators, and suppliers – these are all, in a sense, customers but their relationship is somewhat different. For that reason I refer to them as 'constituents'. They too must be served, but their needs and expectations differ from 'customers'.

There are a number of components critical to corporate quality which must be provided for in any service quality system:

— Management style
— Values
— Behaviour to fellow constituents
— Internal systems

Management style may be autocratic, democratic or anarchic, but whatever the preference it will influence the service quality style of the company as a whole. An autocratic style may ensure conformance with service standards, but is unlikely to result in a flexible response to an unforeseen situation. A *laissez-faire* style may provide high degrees of flexibility, but a lack of consistency in service performance. Whatever the preferred management style it must be congruent with the other parts of the service quality system.

Values will be a major influence on style, behaviour is shaped by values. The driving values of a company may have their roots in times when service quality was less of an issue. In such cases a somewhat painful exercise may be needed to bring about a realignment of values which are more customer sensitive.

Internal systems are also shaped by past prevailing values which may now be outmoded. Such systems range from recruitment and training to accounting and other data processing. Once again, there has to be a review of all systems and the replacement of those which contribute neither to reinforcing competitive quality nor corporate quality. To assist in this process the service quality system needs to call into play four components which knit together the twin strands of competitive and corporate quality:

(1) Service codes
(2) Service contracts
(3) Service standards (and measures)
(4) Service practices

Service codes specify the principles which the company will abide by in providing service to customers and constituents. Examples of codes and the other components to be discussed are given in subsequent sections.

Service contracts specify the reciprocal obligations of both the provider of service and the customer/constituent. It is based on the principle of: 'If you will . . . I will . . .'

Service standards specify the operational limits which should be adhered to in performing specific service tasks. They are normally quantifiable, e.g. 'Letters will be answered within X days of receipt.' Because they are quantifiable, standards can be measured.

Service practices specify types of behaviour which should be used in service encounters. There are usually alternative options provided for, to avoid the danger of 'robotic responses'. Examples of service practices are:

— Forms of greeting
— Conveying that you are listening
— Handling complaints

Service practices are observable and to that extent they can be measured.

5.6 BUILDING THE SERVICE QUALITY SYSTEM

We can look on all the components in Figure 5.1 as building blocks. Before work can begin in cementing them together it is necessary to:

- Define the type of service quality differentiation we want to establish – the service vision
- Determine the gap between the current reality of our service quality and the vision of the future.

5.7 DEVELOPING THE SERVICE VISION

The service vision defines the distinctive characteristics which you wish to be renowned for in the markets you seek to serve. Such characteristics will determine the added-value bestowed on your core product or service by the manner in which it is delivered to customers. Typical characteristics would be:

- Convenience – this has implications for the distribution network and delivery systems
- Reliability – this has implications for quality control and back-up systems
- Exclusiveness – this has implications for location, niche-identification, advertising, pricing, support systems
- Value for money – this has implications for cost structures, product range, competitive advantage protection.

Whatever the distinguishing characteristics which you seek to exhibit, it is necessary to use the model in Figure 5.1 as a template for determining the gap between vision and reality.

5.8 DETERMINING THE VISION-REALITY GAP

The first step in this process is to develop the tools for service quality gap analysis:

(a) Market research of customers' needs and expectations.
(b) Market research of competitor service quality strengths and weaknesses.
(c) In-house research of employees perceptions of service quality strengths and weaknesses.

Market research of customers' needs and expectations can be carried out in a variety of ways:

- Qualitative research – using focus groups to provide insights and perceptions of service quality.
- Interviews with customers on a one-to-one basis.
- Questionnaires – either posted to customers or available at the point of service delivery.
- Complaints/compliments log – recording the stated likes and dislikes of customers.
- Customer roundtables – a gathering of customers arranged by the service provider to air views on service quality.

It is generally desirable to retain an external agency to conduct the market research. This reduces the dangers of bias and ensures that any research based on sampling techniques is statistically reliable.

Market research of competitor service quality strengths and weaknesses can take a number of forms:

(a) Inter-firm comparisons carried out by external agencies.
(b) Analysis of press and trade news.
(c) Use of 'mystery shoppers' who experience the service provided by competitors and report back
(d) Use of own staff to experience the competitive service.
(e) In-house surveys of staff experience and perceptions of competitors.
(f) Debriefing of staff who previously worked for competitors.

In-house research on staff perceptions of their own company's service strengths and weaknesses is very important. People behave in accordance with their perceptions of a situation, therefore, how staff perceive the quality of the service they are providing will greatly influence the actual service experience of the customer. Among the techniques which can be used are:

- Staff roundtables – a gathering of staff from related activities to exchange views on the respective strengths and weaknesses of the service with which they provide one another.
- Workshops – a meeting of staff to identify service quality strengths and weaknesses, suggest possible solutions and devise action plans.
- Quality focus activities – individual and group activities which focus on a specific aspect of service.

- Self audits – a self-administered appraisal of personal strengths and weaknesses in providing service.
- Service assessments – detailed assessment of service quality within a particular unit.

Although the various techniques are described as a prelude to establishing a service quality system, most of them should become an integral part of that system once it is established, as we shall see in subsequent sections.

Service quality is no accident; it is the consequence of a system which draws together a number of components. The manner in which these components interact will determine the two main skeins of service quality:

— Competitive quality
— Corporate quality

5.9 PRACTICES FOR OPTIMISING CUSTOMER SATISFACTION

In seeking to optimise customer satisfaction any service company needs to shift from the traditional management practices which were derived from manufacturing to those which are customer focused. Table 5.1 provides an opportunity to assess how far a company needs to shift from the old ways of managing to what is needed in the 1990s.

There are four components of management to be considered:

(1) Strategy
(2) Style
(3) Systems
(4) Skills

In a sense Table 5.1 ia a blueprint of the changes needed to make each component effective in the enhancement of customer satisfaction.

(1) The strategy component of any such blueprint needs to encompass:

- A worldwide perspective on service quality trends and opportunities affecting the particular service industry.

Table 5.1 Management practices for optimising customer satisfaction

Traditional management practices	Strategy	Customer focused management practices
Optimise profit through maximising margins	0 1 2 3 4 5 6 7 8 9 10	Optimise profit through maximising customer satisfaction
Design and produce product to match internal capabilities	0 1 2 3 4 5 6 7 8 9 10	Design and produce a service quality package to match market needs
Standardise product to maximise efficiency	0 1 2 3 4 5 6 7 8 9 10	Segmentise SQ package to maximise customer satisfaction
Strive to keep ahead of competition	0 1 2 3 4 5 6 7 8 9 10	Strive to keep ahead of customers' needs and expectations
Markets services	0 1 2 3 4 5 6 7 8 9 10	Markets service quality
Corporate objectives state intentions	0 1 2 3 4 5 6 7 8 9 10	Mission statement defines driving values
Strategic thinking is responsibility of top management only	0 1 2 3 4 5 6 7 8 9 10	Strategic awareness is encouraged at all management levels
Service quality is seen as a cost and an add-on	0 1 2 3 4 5 6 7 8 9 10	Service quality is a profit contributor and the core of the business
'Concept of the desirable' is company centred	0 1 2 3 4 5 6 7 8 9 10	'Concept of the desirable' is customer centred

Traditional management practices	Style	Customer focused management practices
Service strategy vision focuses on 'customer care' and 'after service'	0 1 2 3 4 5 6 7 8 9 10	Service Strategy vision focuses on creating a profitable business where service quality imbues every activity
Shaped by tradition and reaction to competitive pressures	0 1 2 3 4 5 6 7 8 9 10	Shaped by global trends and anticipation of customers' needs
Leadership is mastering others	0 1 2 3 4 5 6 7 8 9 10	Leadership is serving others
Managers marshal resources, run things, control other people's behaviour, supervise activities	0 1 2 3 4 5 6 7 8 9 10	Managers satisfy needs, help others grow, control own behaviour, contract for achievement
Management is a 'top-down' activity	0 1 2 3 4 5 6 7 8 9 10	Management is a matrix activity
Discipline aims to punish poor performers	0 1 2 3 4 5 6 7 8 9 10	Discipline aims to help all achieve goals
Motivation is based on fear of failing	0 1 2 3 4 5 6 7 8 9 10	Motivation is based on encouraging success

continued on p. 102

Table 5.1 continued

Traditional management practices	Style	Customer focused management practices
Service is what helps sell the product	0 1 2 3 4 5 6 7 8 9 10	Service is what helps ensure survival
Customers are 'out there'	0 1 2 3 4 5 6 7 8 9 10	Customers are everywhere
Service quality reduces the chances of things going wrong	0 1 2 3 4 5 6 7 8 9 10	Service quality increases the chances of things staying right
Contribution is related to job grade	0 1 2 3 4 5 6 7 8 9 10	Contribution is related to service performance

Traditional management practices	Systems	Customer focused management practices
Ensure efficient administration	0 1 2 3 4 5 6 7 8 9 10	Ensure effective customer service
Internal user friendly	0 1 2 3 4 5 6 7 8 9 10	Customer friendly
Segmented for tracking accountability	0 1 2 3 4 5 6 7 8 9 10	Integrated for customer convenience
Spotlight breakdowns in service	0 1 2 3 4 5 6 7 8 9 10	Facilitate quick recovery from breakdowns in service
Complaints procedure defends company rights	0 1 2 3 4 5 6 7 8 9 10	Complaints procedure puts matters right

Traditional management practices		Customer focused management practices
Feedback concentrates on negatives	0 1 2 3 4 5 6 7 8 9 10	Feedback accentuates positives
Appraisal focuses on reward/punishment and promotion prospects	0 1 2 3 4 5 6 7 8 9 10	Appraisal reinforces performance and career development
Training is course-based and puts in what company decides you need	0 1 2 3 4 5 6 7 8 9 10	Learning is continuous and aims to draw out what company needs
Technology depersonalises systems	0 1 2 3 4 5 6 7 8 9 10	Technology provides opportunity to humanise systems
Quality circles help to compensate service faults of 'systems'	0 1 2 3 4 5 6 7 8 9 10	Service enhancement teams (SETs) help reinforce service effectiveness of 'systems'
	Skills	
Professionalism is based on qualifications	0 1 2 3 4 5 6 7 8 9 10	Professionalism is based on quality of performance
Only 'front line' needs customer contact skills	0 1 2 3 4 5 6 7 8 9 10	Every employee needs some customer contact skills
Competence depends on experience	0 1 2 3 4 5 6 7 8 9 10	Competence shows itself in performance

continued on p. 104

Table 5.1 continued

Traditional management practices	Skills		Customer focused management practices
Technical competence is vital to core activities	0 1 2 3 4 5 6 7 8 9 10		Technical competence is vital in all activities
Behaviour is natural and depends on who we are	0 1 2 3 4 5 6 7 8 9 10		Behaviour is learned and depends on how we manage ourselves
Power is determined by the ability to control and direct the energy of subordinates to get things done	0 1 2 3 4 5 6 7 8 9 10		Power is determined by the ability to release and guide the energy of others to achieve goals
Management skills are action centred	0 1 2 3 4 5 6 7 8 9 10		Management skills are goal/results centred
Service quality skills are derived from production quality techniques	0 1 2 3 4 5 6 7 8 9 10		Service quality skills are derived from psychological techniques
Time management is seen as a technique of organising self and others	0 1 2 3 4 5 6 7 8 9 10		Time management is seen as the means of helping self and others achieve goals
Skilling is about learning	0 1 2 3 4 5 6 7 8 9 10		It is accepted that skilling involves unlearning

- Identification of strategic business units in terms of their impact on customer satisfaction, as well as their profit potential.
- A focus on marketing 'service quality' as well as the 'service product'.
- A plan for using technology to provide a service quality competitive advantage.

(2) The style component of a blueprint needs to provide for:

- The stating of core values and beliefs of the company about customer satisfaction.
- The creation of a 'language' of service to complement the 'language' of the particular industry (see pages 75–84).
- The preparation of the turf for the necessary shifts in culture and traditional norms of behaviour.
- The identification of attitudinal and other blockages to customer satisfaction at individual, team, and departmental levels.
- The reinforcing of the positive driving forces providing the energy to achieve customer satisfaction goals.

(3) The systems component of a blueprint must embrace 'systems' in the broadest sense, but with particular reference to:

- Service delivery
- Service maintenance
- Service audit
- Accountability systems
- Performance data systems
- Feedback systems
- Recognition systems
- Learning systems
- Career progression systems

(4) The skills component of a blueprint will need to aim at ensuring not only the highest levels of technical competence (particularly product knowledge) but also:

- *Service quality management skills*: ability to identify service quality opportunities; set goals, indicators, standards and measures for enhancing service quality, motivate self, individuals and teams by positive reinforcement.

- *Service quality contact skills*: ability to anticipate and respond to needs, expectations and perceptions of customers externally and internally; ability to 'manage' the service interactions; ability to motivate self and others.
- *Service quality team-building skills*: ability to build teams, be a contributing team member, interact effectively with all 'constituencies' of the company.

6 Traditional Approaches to Time and Customer Care

6.1 INTRODUCTION

All service encounters take place in 'real time'. But what real time means to the customer can be very different from what it means to the service provider. Therefore, a critical aspect of customer psychology is the adept use of different concepts of time. Many service providers operate solely on the basis of 'elapsed time' while customers are using different time concepts.

Elapsed time is the number of units of time which pass in a given situation; it can be measured by time-machines such as chronometers, clocks or watches. Other concepts of time are less measurable but are recognised to be of greater significance in determining customer satisfaction. These traditional time concepts are:

— Brain time
— Social time
— Operating time
— Target time

6.2 BRAIN TIME

Brain time (sometimes called 'noetic time') is how the customer senses the time taken to satisfy a need. This is determined by:

(a) the nature of the need;
(b) the urgency of satisfaction;
(c) the extent to which the customer is in control of the situation;
(d) the perceived behaviour of the service provider;
(e) the demands on the customer.

Where the need is trivial in nature the brain time is likely to move faster than elapsed time, particularly if the customer is using the telephone – 'All I want is the price of your product and I've been waiting ages.' The 'ages' of brain time might be two minutes elapsed time. The more significant the need, such as one associated with a life-change, the more slowly will be the passage of brain time, since the pay-off of waiting will be of greater benefit to the customer.

Much will depend on the urgency of the need; a queue for toilets in a restaurant can be felt to have lasted a much longer time than is the actual number of minutes taken. Similarly, the hungry customer will feel that the time taken to deliver the first course of a meal is much longer than that taken to deliver the third course, even though the elapsed times are identical.

Brain time is greatly affected by the amount of control which the customer feels he or she can exercise in the service encounter. Left 'on hold' on the telephone or waiting without warning for a delayed flight to be called are typical situations where the brain time passes slowly. Whereas, given the choice of remaining on hold or calling back the customer who chooses to remain on hold finds that the passage of brain time increases albeit marginally.

As customers we are very sensitive to picking up time signals from the body language of service providers. Signs of lethargy, indifference, slow movements, avoidance of eye contact, chatting inconsequentially to colleagues or other customers all slow down brain time. On the other hand, if staff are seen to be busy, acknowledge the waiting customer, indicate that they want to serve you as soon as possible, brain time moves more quickly and customer satisfaction is increased.

In certain service encounters, customers will be under pressures which affect their brain time. Shopping before going to work or at lunch-time places additional pressures on customers. The service provider should arrange for the maximum staff to be available at such times rather than reduce staff levels or even closing at lunch hours. The greater the personal pressures on a customer, the slower will be the passage of brain time.

6.3   SOCIAL TIME

Different cultures vary in their concept of 'social time'. Punctuality means 'at the appointed time' in Germany, 'up to fifteen minutes after the appointed time' in England, 'up to an hour after the appointed time' in Spain. 'Polite lateness' means being up to an hour late for a drinks party or up to twenty minutes late for a dinner party. Brides are traditionally late for the Christian wedding ceremony, bridegrooms are traditionally early. Attendance at a Royal function in Britain demands that everyone is in attendance well before the Queen arrives, no one leaves until she has departed.

Social time determines not only the degree of punctuality, but the minimum and maximum elapsed time devoted to an event. Annual visits to parents are expected to last at least one day. Staying ten minutes after fellow guests have departed may be social, staying an hour or more is likely to be anti-social. These social time conventions influence customers' perceptions *vis-à-vis* service providers.

Restaurant customers expect to be served if they arrive up to half an hour after the time of their reservation. If this is not acceptable to the service provider the customer should be forewarned. Hotel guests expect to be able to check-in an hour or so after their forecast time of arrival. Each service industry needs to be aware of relevant social time and punctuality applied to it, and either arrange its activities accordingly or disabuse customers of their misconceptions.

When it comes to the duration aspect of social time the service provider needs to be aware of the dominant mindset of the customer and programme activities accordingly. It is social time which is an important element in creating and satisfying customer expectations.

Life-change events such as weddings, funerals or negotiating business finance are meant to last an hour or more. Life-enhancing events such as theatre outings, anniversary dinners, visits to an exhibition are expected to last several hours. Whereas the half-hour play is satisfying on television, a visit to the theatre which lasts only half an hour is unlikely to attract large audiences.

A third dimension of social time which relates to customer psychology is the appropriateness of the hour. This applies to telephone calls and visits to customers' homes. Calls seeking to interest customers in buying a product or service are unlikely to be successful after 9 p.m. or on a holiday. Salesmen at the door are more of an intrusion on a Saturday or Sunday than other days. However, as we have seen in Chapter 1, the concept of being able to call on a service 'any time, any place' is gaining ground. The important factor to keep in mind is that it is customer initiated contacts which are shaping changes in social time.

6.4   OPERATING TIME

Customers expect service providers to be more punctual than themselves. If a store states opening time as 9 a.m. the customer expects that store to be open on the dot, if not before. On the other hand, if the store states that it will close at 5.30 p.m. customers do not expect it to close on the dot. There is much to be said for stores, banks and other service providers advertising opening times which are slightly earlier. The actual opening and closing hours could then vary depending on such factors as weather, number of customers waiting to come in, or availability of staff. Using the ten minute float at each end of the day could significantly enhance customer satisfaction without increasing the hours worked by staff.

A key aspect of operating time is to make customers aware that for every service there are certain operational constraints which impose time limits on providing a service. No matter how efficient, no airline can be punctual if it allows passengers to check-in up to two minutes before take-off. A soufflé cannot be cooked in less than thirty minutes and must be eaten within five minutes of leaving the oven. The clearing of cheques ordinarily requires a minimum number of days. There is a limit to the speed at which petrol can be pumped into a fuel tank without causing a safety hazard. Speed can be an effective competitive weapon (see Chapters 8–9), but there are finite limits to any operation.

There are four trends which are affecting operating times in services:

(1) Automation;
(2) Telecommunications;
(3) Security;
(4) Ageing of the customer population.

Automation reduces operating time by automating and computerising processes. Moving walkways speed passenger movement at airports. Machines provide individually printed documentation. Cheques at payment points need only be signed, the other details being swiftly imprinted. Microwave ovens produce food in minutes. There is, however, a catch – when the computer goes down, the operating time comes to a halt or staggers along at a slow pace.

Telecommunications reduce operating time by sending and receiving data necessary for customer satisfaction. Reservations are confirmed, desired actions initiated, options increased in a fraction of the time taken in previous decades. Once again vulnerability to energy loss, and with it the destruction of important data, is a hazard which the service provider must offset by expensive duplication and back-up systems.

Security in a world of growing crime and terrorism can lengthen operating times and offset the gains of automation and telecommunications. Time locks on bank safes, security screening of passengers and their luggage at airports, employment of security guards in shopping malls, fire and evacuation drills in hotels are all examples of brakes on operating times. Customer acceptance of these practices is high immediately after an outrage but memory fades and with the forgetting comes cognitive distancing – this is the process of separating self from an undesired state. The conviction that 'It could never happen to me' reduces customer tolerance for delays. Unfortunately, security threats and crimes are not going to disappear. Service providers will need to devise ways which counter cognitive dissonance while not scaring the customer. This will call for such practices as:

- Relationship focusing: 'In the interests of your family . . .'
- Bonding: 'All of us travelling today will need to depend on each other in an emergency . . .'
- Alerting: 'Although we take every precaution, these will only be effective if you . . .'
- Social pressuring: 'If you do not comply with these requirements your fellow passengers/guests/customers will be inconvenienced by . . .'

The fourth trend affecting operating times is the ageing of the customer population. As people grow older, they move more slowly, need more explanations, misread signs, mishear directions, visit the toilet more frequently, are more prone to fainting, heart attacks, emotional breakdowns. While the use of transporters at airports, luggage trolleys at stations or chair lifts in restaurants can all help, there is a limit to the cost–benefit of such innovations.

The result of these trends will be the need for companies to invest more in 'customer education', making people aware of the factors which determine the cycles of service and encouraging customers to help make the cycles shorter, smoother or more fast moving. Company secrecy regarding operations has been a prime cause of customers building up unrealistic expectations which lead to dissatisfaction when they are not met.

6.5   TARGET TIME

Customer needs and expectations relate to specific goals or targets. Dates are fixed well ahead for most life-changing events (except death or serious illness). Part of the satisfaction derived from life-enhancing events is looking forward to them. Life-maintaining events are often associated with target dates – bills to be paid, car to be maintained, lawns to be mown or teeth to be checked are but a few activities associated with planned target times.

Target times of customers need to be established as soon as possible by the service provider so that realistic expectations can be set. Both customers and service providers need to agree on target time since the customer may have a self-serving role. A bank manager needs to know the target time for paying back a loan before he can sanction it. The travel agent needs to know the target time for arriving at a destination before she can devise an itinerary. The hotel reservations clerk needs to know both the target times for arrival and departure before confirming a reservation.

Target times provide a trap for the unwary service provider. An essential skill is to wean the customer off unrealistic target times without causing psychic damage. It may be that the customer is willing to pay a premium for meeting a target time which would otherwise be difficult for the service provider.

6.6   TIME AS A SERVICE

Since time immemorial customers have been willing to purchase goods and services which saved them time and energy. From the stage coach to Concorde, people have been willing to buy time shortening of journeys. Convenience foods, disposable nappies, laundrettes, dry cleaners and dating agencies are all examples of time-saving goods and services. Bank loans and mortgages drastically reduce the time required for acquiring possessions or a home.

Time as a service comes in several guises:

— Opportunity time
— Energy time

— Distance time
— Hedonic time.

Opportunity time-services are convenience foods, fast food outlets, dry cleaning and similar services which enable the customer to use the time saved for other purposes such as earning a living. The essence of opportunity time-services is that in the perception of the customer the opportunities for alternative time use are more satisfying than would be time invested in performing the tasks foregone. A person who enjoys cooking will be less inclined to purchase convenience foods than someone who prefers, say, gardening to cooking. As customers get older they require fewer opportunity time services. This is not because they 'have more time on their hands' but because their range of alternative opportunities is reduced. However, with older people the demands for energy-saving time-services increase.

Energy time-services embrace interior decorating, window cleaning, and hotels and restaurants. These services reduce the demands on the physical energy of customers who are able to conserve it or deploy it in more satisfying ways. If energy time services are to succeed, the service provider must ensure that the savings on physical energy are not dissipated by expenditure of psychic energy. If a customer is concerned about the integrity of window cleaners while in their house, this can more than offset the physical benefits of not having to clean the windows.

Distance time-services are of two main types:

— the transport of people and goods;
— telecommunications.

Airlines, railways, buses, couriers and road haulage all fall into the first category. Telephone, radio, television and fax bureaux are examples of the second category.

The attraction of these services is that they condense, often quite dramatically, the time needed to cover distance by alternative means. More than other services, those involved in saving distance time are dependent on technology. The key to their success is technological reliability and the maintenance of back-up systems which reduce the impact of any breakdown.

Customers tend to use immediate comparators in judging the standards of these types of services. Complaints couched in terms of 'with one hour delay at the airport our journey time was doubled' can obscure the fact that any alternative mode of transport would have resulted in a journey of a day or more.

Similarly, if goods are not delivered because the customer was not 'at home' at the time of delivery, the customer tends to focus on the time *spent* collecting the parcel rather than the time saved in the total delivery process. For this reason, companies in the business of delivering goods should build into their costs the price of a phone call to check that the customer is at home and/or deliver in the evenings.

Hedonic time-services are those which aim to provide customers with a 'good time'. Theme parks, theatres, cinemas and holiday hotels are among this type of service. There are three critical factors to be taken into account in providing such services:

(1) Customer characteristics
(2) Reinforcement of the core service
(3) Maintaining positive moods.

Pleasure tastes change between people and ages. With rare exceptions discotheques are unlikely to appeal to the over sixties, nor will formal gardens excite most teenagers. It is therefore essential that providers of hedonic time-services make clear to their customers what they can expect; it may even be necessary to 'warn off' customers who are unlikely to fit in.

People out for a fun time want their sense of fun reinforced while they are enjoying themselves. Thus life-maintaining services such as eating areas, toilets or gift shops should reinforce rather than detract from the enjoyment.

Finally, the concept of hedonic time depends on the maintenance of a joyful mood. Any carping comment by a service provider can break that mood with serious consequences. There is nothing more doleful than people feeling miserable at play.

Whatever the type of service, there is a further aspect which needs to be handled effectively if the experience is to have a positive effect on the psychology of the customer – this is the rhythm of service.

6.7 SERVICE RHYTHMS

Customers' perceptions of service are influenced by the extent to which they and the service provider are 'in rhythm' in the sequencing of events. Many of our body rhythms are linked to magnetic and light emissions from the sun and the moon. The concept of our internal 'metabolic clock' which may be out of phase with the 'time clock' has become familiar as more people fly across time zones on business or pleasure.

Airlines constitute one service industry which has had to take account of the body clock in fixing schedules and arranging catering. Most passengers want to arrive at their destination early in the morning or mid-evening; few passengers want every meal to be breakfast as they fly East to West from Tokyo to London.

Other service industries, particularly retail stores, have to anticipate the rhythm of the seasons in stocking up with clothes. Sunny summers and snowy winters determine the working rhythm of travel companies. Public festivals tied historically to the juxtaposition of sun, moon and earth determine the rhythm of demand for restaurants, greeting cards and alcohol.

6.8 SEASONAL RHYTHMS

Research on the basic DNA string which is the source of life shows that our body clock resets itself daily when strong light enters our eyes. This natural light energy has to be reinforced throughout the day. Unfortunately, modern living with its requirements for work in offices, factories and pleasure in watching television, all in dim light, starves us of this essential energy source and we feel 'out of sorts' or rhythm.

Psychiatrists have identified a body clock malfunction which they call 'seasonal affective disorder' (SAD). This affects people most in the winter, resulting in irritability, anti-social behaviour and withdrawal. Women are much more prone to SAD than men. The use of high levels of artificial light at service delivery points, particularly shops, can go some way to alleviate the symptoms though it will not cure them.

6.9 DAILY RHYTHMS

The British tradition of afternoon tea is related to daily body rhythms. Tea contains traces of a poisonous alkaloid, theophylline. The body can absorb this substance more easily in the late afternoon than at any other hour of the day.

Alcohol consumed in the late hours of the morning causes greater liver damage than at other times. The body clock produces a low tolerance for proteins in the morning and evening hours and for starch in the mornings.

There are more than one hundred rhythms affecting our bodies daily. Many of these influence our behaviour as both customers and service providers.

6.10   INDIVIDUAL RHYTHMS

Biological cycles vary significantly between individuals. The service provider has to be mindful of this in anticipating and responding to customer expectations. The most obvious example is the reproductive cycle of women which, linked to the moon's phases, is ideally a twenty-eight day cycle, but may vary between twenty-one or thirty or more days. Linked to this monthly rhythm is the life-rhythm of the menopause, the onset and duration of which can vary by years from one woman to another. The observant service provider can look for visual clues in seeking to empathise with customers undergoing such rhythmic changes.

6.11   RHYTHM PACING

Service providers who can synchronise with the rhythmic needs of the customer will achieve higher levels of customer satisfaction.

Where the dominant mindset is life changing, customers will generally want the initial service encounters to move at a relatively slow pace. This enables them to absorb key information and check their understanding. Time indicators are extremely important. The service provider should check the time-span expectation of the customer and sequence the service encounter accordingly. Key phrases are:

- 'How much time do *we* have?'
- 'I suggest we spend (specified time) and see how far we get.'
- 'Let's spend (a short specified time) today setting out the main issues so that we can concentrate on them (in due course).'

The service provider should never indicate that a time-span will be determined *solely* by his/her availability.

Where the dominant customer mindset is life enhancement, the primary focus of the customer will be on immediate or potential gratification of need. There is therefore a premium on signalling at an early stage in the service encounter, whether or not the service provider can give an indication of satisfying the desired gratification. Key phrases are:

- 'I'm sure we can meet your needs if you give me the necessary details.'
- 'When's the latest time you want this by?'
- 'Let me check availability now, then we can complete the paperwork.'
- 'Today's Monday, I'll have everything in order by _____ and you can collect it on _____. Is that satisfactory?'

Life-maintaining mindsets can be more difficult to pace since they vary in type, between regular, seasonal and impulse.

Regular chores will include:

(a) Daily travel to and from work.
(b) Weekly grocery shopping.
(c) Monthly meal with fellow members of a club.
(d) Six monthly check-up at the dentist.
(e) Annual account review meeting with the bank manager.

Seasonal chores will consist of:

(a) Christmas shopping.
(b) Preparing car for winter.
(c) Purchasing goods and services for spring cleaning.
(d) Buying clothes for children returning to school.

Impulse chores will take many forms such as:

(a) Stopping at a service station to fill up with petrol.
(b) Catching a taxi instead of waiting for a bus.
(c) Having a snack because you are hungry.
(d) Buying from a shop because you have just remembered a need.

Whatever the type of service encounter, those relating to life maintenance are the most prone to mismatches between 'elapsed time' and 'brain time'. The service provider needs constantly to bear in mind that chores are forced choices. The saying, 'how time flies when you are enjoying yourself' should be changed to 'how time slows down when you are involved in a chore'.

This 'time-drag' syndrome can be modified in various ways:

- Automation – the use of cash dispensers by banks; self-service pumps at petrol stations.
- Diversion – use of video screens and other distractions to alleviate boredom in queues.
- Information – announcements or notices informing customers of time they have to wait to reach the service delivery point.
- Alleviation – provide opportunity for customer to undertake other activities without losing place in queue, for example, issuing tickets with sequential numbers and serving in number order.
- Segregation – provide quick service check-outs for customers with few goods.

None of these alternatives is foolproof. Cash dispensers break down; video messages which have frequent repetition can exacerbate the 'brain time' of waiting; customers lose tickets or abuse the quick service 'break point'. Despite these disadvantages, the service provider who can help the customer align 'elapsed time' and 'brain time', or even better make the 'brain time' move faster than the real time, is on to a winner in pacing service encounters.

6.12   CONCLUSION

For many years, manufacturers and service providers have used 'time' as a means of attracting customers to their products. Table 6.1 gives examples of typical time-related advertisements.

A time dimension has long been recognised in many products and services. What is now apparent is that in terms of customer care, time is the product or service. This calls for fresh thinking about how as customers we perceive the time dimension. New concepts of time Zones and time States are coming into play.

Life is tiny bits of time which each of us shapes into unique mosaics of living. Helping customers shape their mosaics into the desired patterns lies at the heart of Customer Care. How we can bring this about is the subject of Part II, to which we now turn.

Table 6.1 Advertisements using 'time' as a selling aid

Product/Service	Copy message
Language course	'I learnt a new language in seven days'
Watch	'What time is it? An eternity'
Cooker	'Here's why – Hi-speed is simply the best cooker in the world.' (Cooks conventionally in shorter time than competitors)
Decorative plate for anniversary of Battle of Britain	'Our finest hour'
Hi-fi system	'It's not new – just improved'
Face cream	'Banish ugly ageing skin blemishes'
Hair removal by electrolysis	'At last, effective electrolysis at home . . .'
China ornament	'Reflections of a more elegant age'
Marmalade	'No day that starts with . . . marmalade can be entirely bad'
Hand tools	'Guaranteed 25 years'
Lager	'For generations – lager has been part of the noble art of beer drinking . . .',
Camera	'To preserve his best features you need ours'
Beer	'One pint is worth a month of Sundays'

continued on p. 120

Table 6.1 continued

Product/Service	Copy message
China ornament	'The magic hour'
Hi-fi and video equipment	'The future is here'
Bed	'For those planning to retire early'
Liqueur	'And the evening began'
School fees	'Don't be a dunce, plan your child's education now'
Watch	'Timeless elegance'
Whale and Dolphin conservation	'Their future is now in your hands'
Automobile	'The new generation of . . .'
Vitamin tablets	'Ageing increases the risk of certain diseases'
Private aircraft	'The opportunities in today's Europe will go to those who can get there first'
Air parcel service	'Your parcel has started to clear Customs, before it's cleared for take off'
Camera	'Looking back to 1992'
Airline	'Solar system'
Facsimile machine	'How useful will your fax be in a few years if it isn't a . . .'
Automobile	'The car for the 90s'
Automobile	'The shape of the 90s'

Part II

The Subconscious Elements of Customer Care Psychology

7 Time – What Every Customer Wants

7.1 INTRODUCTION

Time is the most precious possession which is shared equally by mankind and womankind; the distinction is not a bow to feminism, but a highlighting of the different time perspectives of the male and female in any society.

Boys mature at puberty at different rates from girls. Women tend to marry at a younger age than do men. Men generally die at an earlier age than women; so for biological reasons, although in any one day, week, month or year, men and women share the same measured amount of time, over a century men have less time than women.

While time is shared in common, it is paradoxically the most individual phenomenon known to the human race. Each person spends their total time in different ways. Though everyone in a situation such as flying across the Atlantic shares a common experience of flying time, each person from moment to moment is undergoing a unique blending of other 'times'. Some may be reading, others eating or sleeping, or chatting; all are thinking different thoughts – reminiscing about the past, speculating about the future, each in a different 'time world'.

Helping individuals make what they perceive to be the best use of their precious time is the primary purpose of every manufacturing and service industry. No matter what the tangible product or the intangible service may be, what the customer is buying is time.

'Caring for customers' comes down in the final analysis to caring for their time. Identifying the type of time the customer wants and providing it in a manner which not only meets but outmatches that want, is the basis of customer psychology. In later chapters, I shall describe how time is the *only* enduring competitive weapon and how it can be used to secure competitive advantage. But to do this it is necessary to provide the building blocks of time, using labels which at first sight may seem unusual. This is inevitable when describing a revolutionary new way of thinking about customers.

7.2 THE BUILDING BLOCKS

Let us begin by reminding ourselves what is a customer – an individual who has a need which he or she seeks to satisfy by choosing a supplier of a product or service most appropriate to the need and at a price that the customer can afford. The essence of being a customer, as distinct from a consumer, is the exercise of free will in the process of choice. The essential factor in making the choice is the balance of earning time and purchased time.

The price of a product or service may be uniform in terms of money units, but its cost varies significantly in terms of time units. A car may have a price tag of £6000 but its cost to a stockbroker in the City of London could be a one hour unit of work-time, whereas for a janitor it could represent more than a hundred one-hour units of work-time. In effect, any transaction between a provider of a product/ service and a customer is a trade-off between one category of time for another.

Although the so-called Customer Revolution of the mid-1980s has attached the label 'customer' to all categories of users and consumers, this is misleading. Inmates of prisons are not 'customers' exercising free choice; they have been denied control over their use of time. In fact the phrase that a prisoner has been 'given time' means the opposite of what it states. (The death penalty is the ultimate punishment since it terminates time for the condemned prisoner.)

As an aside, the concept of fines as an alternative to prison is a stark illustration of trading off work-time against custodial time. Recent cases of malfeasance by millionaire financiers on Wall Street and in the City of London illustrate a somewhat new legal precedent of fixing a fine to the proceeds of a period of work-time as against custodial time. For some, a year out of prison has been deemed to be worth much more than for others.

So the first building block is that the customer is always trading one category of time for another. This is the 'time exchange balance'. The more the customer perceives that the balance is equal or weighted in his/her favour, the higher will be the level of customer satisfaction. Creating this perception calls into play customer care psychology.

The adroit use of Customer Care Psychology requires that there is a clear understanding by the producer of a product or provider of a service between psychic time and purchasable time.

Psychic time-zones form the second building block; this label describes different perceptions of 'time' which each of us experience in our minds as we live from day to day, year to year. Often we are consciously aware of these zones, but they also operate at subconscious levels in our assessment of customer care – the most important psychic-time-zones are:

— Biological
— Chronological
— Communications
— Durability
— Family
— Leisure
— Private
— Provisioning
— Ritual
— Survival
— Travel
— Waiting
— Work
— Worship

In addition to these 'psychic time-zones' there are two more types of time which provide the context within which we live and switch zones; universal time and global time.

Universal time is the physical, astronomical phenomenon governing all things in the cosmos. It has been studied through the ages by seers and scientists seeking to explain its purpose, laws and future development. Unfortunately, it is not possible to give finite answers about the infinite.

In his book, *A Brief History of Time* (Bantam Press, 1988), Professor Stephen W. Hawking concludes: 'if we do discover a complete theory it should in time be broadly understood by everyone, not just a few scientists . . . if we find the answer . . . it would be the ultimate triumph of human reason – for then we would know the mind of God.' My aim is far less ambitious. It is to know the mind of customers; universal time has little to contribute to that.

Global time is more important to customer care psychology since it provides the temporal context for all psychic time-zones. Clocks, watches and calendars are all instruments of global time. We need always to remind ourselves that 'time', as we know it and measure it, was invented by man and can be changed at any time. In fact, we have grown up with the concept of 'Summer Time' which leads us to subtract and then 'replace' one hour on two dates of each year.

We will return to the concept of global time, but for the present we need to consider the next building block.

The third building block is the concept of the time-state. Within each psychic time-zone, individuals, be they performing the role of customers or not, are psychologically attuned to a time-state. This influences their behaviour, perceptions and sense of priorities. For example, in the biological time-zone an individual may be eating; this is a time-state which is determining his or her behaviour (consuming food). However, the individual may be on a train while eating, thereby being in two psychic time-zones, biological and travel, simultaneously. In the latter zone the individual is in a train journeying time-state; this influences expectations of the time to be spent on the journey *vis-à-vis* alternative forms of travel.

Let us imagine that the individual eating on the train is reading a book during the meal. This means that the passenger is in the leisure time-zone and in a reading time-state within that zone. What the passenger is doing is 'layering', overlapping one time-zone within another. We shall return to the concept of layering (see Chapter 8); for the moment let us concentrate on the rail passenger eating and reading.

If the train is running to time; if the meal is well cooked and well served; if the book is a 'good read', the passenger will be enjoying the benefits of positive time-states in all three zones. On the other hand, if the train is delayed or the meal of low quality or the book boring, the level of customer satisfaction will drop as the passenger moves from a positive to a negative time-state.

A positive time-state in any zone enhances customer satisfaction, while a negative time state in any zone reduces it. The challenge of customer care psychology is to accentuate the positives and eliminate the negatives in all time-zones. Unfortunately, it is not easy to identify the time-states within which the customer is operating. This is because in every psychic time-zone a customer is making choices and judging results in terms of one or more dominant life needs. This brings us to the fourth building block of the new customer psychology.

7.3 DOMINANT LIFE NEEDS

As we have seen in Part I, all of us are influenced by only three types of need:

(1) Life maintaining
(2) Life enhancing
(3) Life changing

Life-maintaining needs are the most numerous; they range from responding to bodily functions to cashing a cheque, to having clothes dry cleaned, to eating something to 'keep us going'. Many life-maintaining needs can be satisfied swiftly; a significant number are externally imposed and are perceived as chores. Given free choice, few people would enjoy paying bills, filling up their cars with fuel, or returning faulty goods. The fulfilling of life-maintaining needs is, as we shall see, often accompanied by a negative time-state. Service providers can respond to meeting life-maintaining needs by undertaking the chore on behalf of the customer (e.g. office cleaning) or reducing the chore element (e.g. providing distractions while queuing). Many manufactured goods are aimed at reducing or eliminating chores. These range from dishwashers to self-cleaning ovens; from waste disposal units to paper shredders. Life maintaining-needs *have* to be satisfied to live in a civilised world.

Life-enhancing needs are, on the other hand, largely discretionary. These needs relate to our desire for a better life-style, for a more enjoyable use of our time. Holidays, acquiring a new car, going to the theatre, treating ourselves to a luxury, throwing a party, each of these examples highlight the characteristics of life-enhancement needs:

- Discretionary – we don't have to satisfy them.
- Enjoyable -- we aim to be in a positive time-state when satisfying the need.
- High expectancy of outcome – we look forward to life-enhancing events with high hopes.

When any one of these characteristics is missing the customer moves from a positive to a negative time-state. A party one feels forced to give or attend is not life enhancing, but life maintaining (maintaining relationships). A play we do not enjoy becomes a bore. Events which do not come up to expectations are disappointments and thus move us into the negative time-states.

Providers of services and products aimed at satisfying life-enhancing needs have to pay particular attention to managing expectations, thus reducing the impact of disappointment. They must also be sensitive to vicarious satisfaction; parents take their offspring to circuses so that the children will enjoy it; we give presents which will provide joyful satisfaction to the receiver rather than ourselves, our joy coming from the expression of satisfaction by others. Pleasant surprises (see Chapter 4) can reinforce satisfaction of life-enhancement needs, unpleasant surprises negate any positive benefits of life enhancement.

Life-change needs are less common than the other two, but their satisfaction is usually more vital. The most significant life changes we encounter are:

- Birth
- Marriage
- Graduation
- First job
- Career change
- Birth of children
- Divorce
- Starting own business
- Retirement
- Change of home location
- Death of loved ones
- Onset of deadly disease
- Major injury
- Major medical operation
- Death

The characteristics of life changes are:

(a) They present change in self-image, role relationships.
(b) They often require choice between two or more undesirable alternatives. (Choosing between obvious 'good' and obvious 'bad' is not a difficult choice to make.)
(c) They can have a significant impact on others.

Life changes are often accompanied by ritual which has its roots in long-established traditions. These can define such matters as:

— timing of events (Christians cannot marry in church at certain times of the year);
— dress (black ties at funerals);
— pacing of events (no one wants a five minute wedding breakfast);

— location (marriages can only take place on certain premises, bodies can only be buried in cemeteries);
— food (menus for Passover, Easter, Christmas, are well defined);
— precedence in location (who sits where, who supports which part of a coffin).

Those involved in satisfying life change needs have to be:

(a) well qualified in a profession (doctor, lawyer, priest);
(b) knowledgeable about protocol (funeral undertaker, wedding caterer, master of ceremonies);
(c) sensitive to the mood of the event (no laughing at funerals);
(d) conversant with legal and regulatory requirements (registrars of births, marriages and deaths; doctors and bankers working within ethical codes).

To sum up, within each psychic time-zone a customer, at any point in time, is living in one or more time-states which in most cases will be perceived and experienced as positive or negative. The impact of a particular time-state and how it is perceived will be determined by the dominant life need which the customer is seeking to satisfy. There are three types of life need:

(1) Life maintaining
(2) Life enhancing
(3) Life changing

Mastery of the customer care psychology requires the ability to identify the time-states within the various time-zones in which the customer is operating, then to accentuate the positive states and eliminate the negative ones by anticipating and satisfying the appropriate dominant life need.

We shall shortly turn to a study of each psychic time zone and its family of time-states. Analysis of these will highlight opportunities for using customer care psychology in a creative, ethical manner.

Before concentrating on the concept of time as the core factor in customer care psychology we shall consider the evolution of global time which governs our every action. In so doing we will come to recognise that like the other forms of time discussed in subsequent chapters, global time is not a natural phenomenon, but is man made.

7.4   THE DEVELOPMENT OF GLOBAL TIME

Time is the one possession which all beings have in equal amounts at any given instant. The Australian aborigine, the American banker and the Icelandic fisherman all share Time in equal measure as a physical phenomenon. However, when it comes to time as a psychological phenomenon things are very different. Each of us seeks in various ways to extend our *share* of time since we know that though time will continue indefinitely, we shall not.

Since the dawn of civilisation, to coin a time cliché, Man has sought to package time. Though time as we know it was first packaged by Egyptian astronomers many thousands of years before Christ, repackaging has recurred well into the twentieth century. The Egyptians, from their studies of the movement of the Moon, stars and Sun in relation to Earth, devised cyclical time by creating the concept of a twenty-four hour day lasting from sunrise to sunrise. Using water clocks, sundials and shadow clocks the twenty-four hours were divided into two periods of twelve hours, each subdivided into units of one hour.

Babylonian astronomers around 2000 BC refined the Egyptian 'package' by devising two larger cyclical units, the seven day week and the thirty day month. Influenced by their habit of calculating in multiples of sixty, the Babylonians went on to a further repackaging of time in terms of dividing hours into minutes and seconds.

Over the centuries the Greeks and Romans developed the concept of the year based on the movement of the Earth around the Sun. The number of lunar months in the year varied until 46 BC when Julius Caesar defined a year as comprising twelve months. As the years passed, the Julian calendar began to cause problems for those engaged in the two major industries in Europe – agriculture and the Church. The latter was the first major service industry providing not only spiritual guidance, but education and medical services.

7.5   THE IMPACT OF THE CHURCH

The trouble with the Julian calendar was that the 365.25 days which it covered was too long by about twelve minutes. The consequence over the centuries was that the dates marking the seasons of the year had shifted by almost two weeks by 1582. This meant that key dates for farming, tax gathering and religious festivals were becoming out of joint. Pope Gregory XIII, a visionary, could foresee the situation becoming worse over future centuries and so promulgated a new calendar by decreeing that the day after 4 October 1582 be defined as 15 October.

Not everyone was willing to accept the Gregorian time package. Resistance was based on socio-psychological factors rather than scientific evidence. Reactions foreshadowed many factors which still need to be borne in mind by those seeking to profit by repackaging time.

Resistance by the newly formed Protestants to papal power resulted in Britain continuing with the Julian time package until 1752. By then it was necessary to make an eleven day adjustment instead of the nine days, two centuries earlier. This resulted in riots with fatalities as workers in the emerging manufacturing industries felt that they had not only lost eleven days of their lives but also nine days pay.

Even today, the Gregorian calendar is not in use across the globe. Muslims subscribe to a lunar calendar and the Chinese have a different sequencing of the start of each year. Orthodox Christians celebrate Easter at a different date from other Christian sects.

Over the centuries various attempts have been made to repackage the week. The ten day week of the ancient Greeks was revived by the French Revolutionaries of the eighteenth century who for a short spell tried to decimalise time. More recently, the Soviet Revolutionaries introduced a five day week, then extended it to six and finally settled for a seven day week in 1940.

7.6 THE IMPACT OF INDUSTRY

While there have been religious and political motives for packaging time, another cause has been the impact of industry and commerce. The development of the week has no basis in astronomy, but it provided a means for the first major service industry, the Catholic Church, to present its 'customers' with a range of spiritual and temporal services on a regular basis.

Similarly, the first automation of a service, the application of the steam engine to travel, brought into prominence the importance of the minute, as railways began to provide scheduled services and published detailed timetables. As we approach the third millennium (another way of packaging time), the millisecond comes into play in such industries as financial services, where profit can be made by being in advance of the competition in dealing across the globe in miniscule units of time.

History provides clues to service industries today on how time can be viewed as a product. In the twentieth century there has been a move from the packaging of time in terms of units of measurement to its packaging as a product which provides opportunities for added-value. To take full advantage of those opportunities every service industry has to rethink concepts of time, since in the final analysis, no matter what it is selling, what its customers are buying is time.

The concept of global time-zones, is a relatively recent phenomenon which had its roots in the United States of America. As pioneers moved across that vast continent from east to west, each large city followed Boston time which was derived from the Harvard Observatory. By the mid-nineteenth century there were upwards of fifty time-zones, causing some confusion for rail travellers and farmers reading weather forecasts based on different time bases; sometimes clock-time, sometimes by the position of the sun. 'High noon' in Chicago could be significantly different in time from 'high noon' in Colorado.

The Weather Bureau pressed for a more standard approach to time across the nation, against opposition from intellectuals and writers such as Herman Melville and Nathaniel Hawthorne. There were many people in rural areas who felt that standardisation was an affront to nature and its relationship with time. Railways, however, once again influenced concepts of time to convenience their passengers boarding at different points across the country. In 1883, the major transcontinental railways agreed on the four standard-time-zones which still operate today in the USA.

The boundaries and extent of each standard-time-zone is not based on a deep geophysical study; railways simply defined each boundary at the places where they were already stopping to refuel and change drivers. In a sense, this was the first recognition of a 'customer time-zone'; determined by the prowess of the steam locomotive to transport passengers and freight from one place to another. Once again, as in the development of the week, the 'time-zone' was a purely pragmatic device related more to the need to provide a service and to calculate costs, than to be consistent with the theories of Copernicus, Galileo or Albert Einstein.

7.7 CONCLUSION

Global time is, in fact, a mixture of three types of measurable units:

(1) Astronomically based – derived from the work of the Egyptians and Babylonians.
(2) Customatised – created to indicate significant passages of time and provide a basis for determining time-cycles for events.
(3) Symbolic – devised to signify the longer term passage of time from an event whose significance transcends individual experience, and is therefore celebrated or remembered by all those whose lives have been affected in some ways by the event.

Figure 7.1 gives examples of the various units which together provide the context within which we experience different types of psychic time-zones in our day-to-day activities.

The psychic time-zones of customer care psychology share some of the features of standard time-zones; man-made boundaries sometimes arbitrary, provide a device for enhancing personal convenience and customer satisfaction.

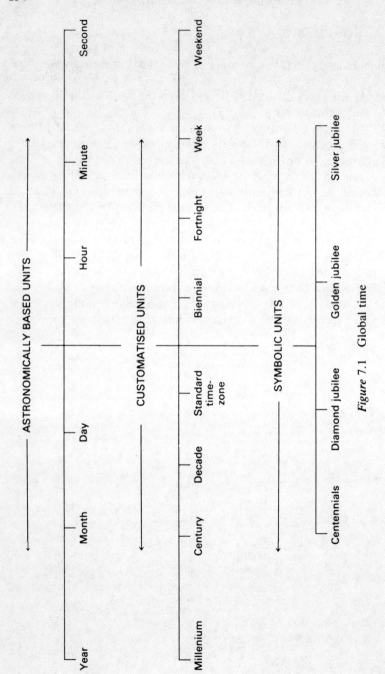

Figure 7.1   Global time

8 Customer Care Time-shaping

8.1 INTRODUCTION

Time-shaping is the ability of the service provider to work with the customer to ensure that he or she is maximising the experience which is being provided by the service company.

There are four types of time-shapers:

(1) Diversions
(2) Compressing
(3) Layering
(4) Contra-flowing

Used skilfully and sensitively these devices will significantly enhance customer satisfaction. Used without careful thought and planning they will have an adverse effect on customer care psychology.

8.2 TIME-DIVERSION

Used properly diversions can be effective in helping a customer to shift from one psychic time-zone to another, or to move from a negative time-state to a positive one within the same zone. Video displays when queuing or waiting at stations or airports are an example of a diversion which takes the customer's mind off the negative state of waiting, and may stimulate a mind to move into another psychic time-zone, say, biological, by focusing on some aspect of health.

Games to pass the time on long journeys, give-away balloons at garages, free coffee while waiting in a bank, magazines in dentists' waiting rooms, are all examples of diversions. Their aim is to take the mind of the customer away from a negative time-state into a positive one in the same or different psychic time-zones.

Small pleasant surprises or treats are other types of diversions. A rose presented to a female partner while leaving a restaurant can divert the mind of the host from the size of the bill. Less cynically, it can help shape the evening by shifting perceptions from an act of eating to an act of loving.

Interruptions are negative diversions; they shift the customer from where she or he wants to be, physically or psychologically, to an undesired state. Journeys that are interrupted because of a break-down; family meals that are interrupted by a telephone 'cold call'; meals that are interrupted by overattentive waiters ready to pounce to light the customer's cigarette – all these are examples of negative diversions.

As in all other aspects of customer care psychology the aim must be to accentuate the positive diversions and to avoid or eliminate the negative ones.

An increasingly common type of time-diversion is the use of music when 'on hold' awaiting a response on the telephone. When on hold customers feel that they have been 'waiting ages' when they have been 'waiting minutes'. Filling the waiting gap with music may not have the desired effect on customer psychology because different types of music have the following physiological effects:

- Increased bodily metabolism;
- Enhanced perception;
- Accelerated respiratory rate;
- Altered muscular energy;
- Raised or lowered blood pressure;
- Altered blood circulation;
- Lowered threshold for various sensory stimuli.

Music can facilitate seduction, rouse political and religious emo-tions, lull a child to sleep or send parents into a frenzy. Dance music such as waltzes, quicksteps, foxtrots and orchestral marches produce predominantly muscular responses; hearing such music, we tap with our feet or move our hands in rhythm. Much modern music has respiratory and cardiovascular effects; it gets us moving, either in a frenzy of despair, or an ecstasy of fulfilment, depending on our age and disposition.

Customer care psychology suggests that the use of music in stores, restaurants, aircraft, stations and other points of service delivery needs careful selection if it is to have the desired effect.

For most customers, music belongs to the leisure time-zone. Trying to shift the customer there from the waiting time-zone is impossible to achieve in a short time-span, as is usually the case when put 'on hold'. Imposed music, whereby the customer has to listen to it or lose contact on the phone, can be a negative diversion rather than a positive one. A useful approach would be to give the customer a choice, 'Do you want to hold on?' 'Would you prefer silence or music?' By this means the customer would be shaping the waiting time.

8.3 TIME-COMPRESSING

Time-compressing is a device for increasing customer satisfaction by making available, in a short period of time, a range of experiences. Examples are:

- One/two day trips by Concorde to:
  Pyramids
  Bolshoi Ballet in Moscow
  Summer Lights in Lapland.
- Christmas shopping, show, candlelit dinner and overnight hotel in a capital city.
- Opportunity to see a range of cars at a motor show.
- Opportunity to see an extensive collection of one particular artist at a major retrospective exhibition.
- Crash course on some subject.
- Ability to view more than one TV channel simultaneously.
- Haircut, manicure and pedicure at same time.

Time-compressing requires careful planning on the 'theme' which will link the various activities, otherwise the customer may perceive them as being out of sync. In particular, the activities should be in the same psychic time-zone in order to make a positive impact on customer psychology. The essence of time-compressing is that it enables a customer to satisfy a number of related needs in a shorter time than the competition. Meeting customer needs at a speed comfortable to the customer is the major determinant of success or failure in evaluating time-compressing.

Time-compressing products can be found in virtually every psychic time-zone:

- Instant coffee, tea, quick boiling rice, instant desserts and microwave ovens are all examples of time-compressing products in the biological time-zone. They reduce the preparation time for food and drink.
- The telephone in all its forms, the fax machine, photocopier, and above all the computer are all examples of time-compressing products in the communications time-zone which influence behaviour in other zones.
- Cars, trains, aircraft and ferries are all time-compressing products in the travel time-zone.
- Polaroid cameras and video camrecorders are time-compressors in the chronological time-zone, permitting us to review a past event more quickly than ever before. These can have a major impact in the family and leisure time-zones, permitting significant events to be 'staged' as well as recorded for posterity. No longer need the blushing bride worry about how she will appear in the wedding photographs, no longer need the proud parent be upset at the pouting child in the photograph specially taken for grandma. Instant retakes will ensure a smile – or else!
- Mobile homes, sun-tanning machines and gas-fired barbecues are but a few examples of time-compressors in the leisure zone. Time-compression has a marked effect on customer care psychology in this zone because it reduces the time spent on the chore of preparation, leaving more time to enjoy the event.

Perhaps the most intriguing example of a successful time-compressing product is *Readers Digest*. Its format has remained virtually unchanged since it was founded in New York by De Witt and Lila Wallace in 1922. Every issue contains around thirty articles, one for each day of the month in question. Most of these articles are condensed from over 500 publications which are surveyed each month. This enables the reader to 'keep up to date' on a host of subjects. The benefits of time-compression are enjoyed by over 16 million customers across the globe and millions more readers, making *Readers Digest* the most successful general interest magazine in the world.

Companies which can appeal to customers' needs for time-compression can enjoy a bright future. The secret is striking the right formula; if *Readers Digest* was to attempt further compression by producing sixty articles per month it is unlikely that it would retain its readership.

8.4 TIME-LAYERING

Time-layering is a process whereby a service provider adds additional services to its core time product from other psychic time-zones which can be experienced simultaneously, thus enhancing customer satisfaction. Examples are:

- Airlines' core time-zone is travel time. They can layer:
  Leisure time through audio and visual entertainment.
  Work time through the provision of business equipment and air to ground telephones.
  Biological time through the provision of food and drink.
  Provisioning time through selling duty free goods and arranging mail order.
  Communications time by enabling passengers to use air to ground telephones.

- Hotels' core time-zone may be either work time or leisure time. They can layer:
  Work time on leisure time or vice versa.
  Family time by catering for significant family events.
  Provisioning time by having a range of shops on the premises.
  Ritual time by catering for significant life events and exclusive groups such as Masons or Lions.
  Workshop time by providing a meditation room where religious services can be held.

- Department stores' core time-zone is provisioning time. They can layer:
  Family time by taking care/entertaining children while parents shop.
  Leisure time by having 'fun' promotions and special events.
  Biological time by providing restaurants and toilets; also hairdressing and beauty treatment.
  Chronological time by displaying the latest fashions in clothes and accessories.
  Travel time by providing swift and safe lifts, escalators and moving walkways.
  Worship time by providing meditation room.

- Cinemas' core time-zone is leisure time. They can layer:
  Biological time by providing food, drink and toilets.

Provisioning time by having shops on the premises.
Family time by supervising children in one cinema while parents are in another and, possibly, grandparents in yet a third.
Chronological time by providing previews of future films.

Whereas time-compressing is a time-shaper within one time-zone, time-layering enables a customer to shape time in a number of time-zones concurrently. It can be a formidable competitive weapon in any service industry.

Time-layering also relates to products; the combined washing machine and spindryer; the radio-cassette alarm that makes tea; and above all the motor car.

Cars are designed primarily for the travel time-zone. Over the decades there have been enormous advances in car design and performance. The ability to transport individuals from one place to another has, however, been limited by the law and by the volume of road traffic. Although motor manufacturers could enhance the speed of their vehicles, they have been forced to move away from the travel time-zone into other zones to remain competitive. The most important are:

— Biological time-zone – increased attention to safety. Seat belts do not enhance the performance of a car, but they do reduce the chances of injury and death. Unleaded petrol does not enhance performance, but it is less harmful to health.
— Durability time-zone – reduction of corrosion, longer lasting seat covers, easy to repair/replace parts are examples of advances in this time-zone.
— Leisure time-zone – stereo-cassette players, radios, and TV for passengers are examples of making travel by car more enjoyable rather than more speedy.
— Work time-zone – car phones, portable fax machines and voice activated personal computers are but a few examples of converting a car into a 'work station'.

Looking ahead, built in microwave ovens, special non-drip cups (such as babies now use) and video-cassette players for passengers will combine to make the motor car truly a 'time-machine' where customers can reach their destination and simultaneously have been in several time-zones.

Perhaps one of the most outstanding 'time-layering' products is the

Sony Walkman. It allows people to perform chores, to walk, cycle, drive, sunbathe, bath, and attend to bodily functions while keeping up with the latest news, listening to favourite music, learning a language, or being briefed on the latest management technique. The success of the Walkman reinforces the theory that customers seek 'time' as both a product and a service. 'Time-layering' is a major key to success in customer care.

8.5 TIME CONTRAFLOWS

Time contraflows are useful devices for increasing customer satisfaction either by extending product life or making a product available earlier than is the norm. Examples are:

(a) Labelling a range of clothes, pens, watches as 'Classic' thus extending their appeal by flowing against the latest short-lived fashion.
(b) Long-life milk extends the appeal of an otherwise short-lived fresh product.
(c) All day breakfasts – extending the opportunities to sell what was formerly a morning only product.
(d) Beaujolais Nouveau – going contrary to the long-term appeal of vintage wines.
(e) Cornflakes for dessert – extending the opportunities to serve a hitherto breakfast-only food.
(f) Fizzy drinks for breakfast – extending the opportunities to serve at breakfast what was previously a non-breakfast drink.
(g) Morgan cars – providing a new car whose appeal is that is old fashioned.
(h) Revivals of plays, musicals and films which appeal to nostalgia as distinct from being recognised classics.

Time contraflowing will become increasingly important as we approach the year 2000. The advent of the third millennium will influence customers to hark back to the 'good old days'. This is because, unlike a new century, there is no one alive who has experienced entering a millennium – fear of the unknown will reinforce the desire for the solace of the 'known'.

Ecological considerations will also play their part in attracting customers to 'the old ways' of doing things. The whole 'organic food' movement is an example of a massive time 'contraflow'.

Many supermarkets will be introducing lines which revert to traditional methods of production in order to provide better flavour. Using old recipes they will strive to recapture the 'traditional' flavour and consistency lost in mass production.

Longer maturing times for cheese and more labour intensive methods of curing bacon will result in higher prices. Although the food may be 'old fashioned' its marketing will be up to date. 'Farmhouse', 'hand-picked', 'traditional'; and 'golden age' are but a few of the words used to market these 'new old' products. Their packaging in recycled brown paper bags will reinforce the 'contraflow' effect.

Contraflowing will only work in the end if the customer believes in the integrity of the product or service. Should a perception of gimmickry or exploitation develop in the mind of the customer, contraflowing will be counter-productive.

8.6   ENTERTAINMENT IN THE AIR – AN EXAMPLE OF TIME SHAPING

A survey of airline passengers in mid-1990 by British Airways, TWA and Cathay Pacific revealed that comedy is king when it comes to in-flight entertainment.

Of the 4000 passengers interviewed, 58 per cent watched some or all of the video/television entertainment on their flight. Half of those preferred comedy to the other categories which in descending order of preference were:

— Daily news
— Documentary
— Destination video
— Weekly news
— Wildlife
— Drama
— Cartoons
— Business news.

Men preferred sport and women drama, otherwise there were no gender differences.

Cultural differences do, however, present problems in finding films with global appeal. Films have to be edited to avoid offending or worrying passengers. In the USA, airlines require stricter editing than elsewhere with swearing and frontal nudity being cut out, though violence is allowed to remain. European airlines are more tolerant about bad language and nudity, but restrict violent scenes to the minimum. When it comes to the Middle East, violence remains, but any sexual scenes, even a chaste kiss, are excised.

In the 1990s, airlines will be investing more than ever in providing a wider choice of viewing and allowing passengers to shape their viewing time as they wish. For example, British Airways will provide First Class passengers with a choice of 100 movies on their own personal video system. Club Class passengers will be able to watch a six channel video system.

As distinct from 'canned' entertainment, more airlines flying jumbo-sized aircraft may follow the lead of Virgin Atlantic which regularly provides live entertainment ranging from jugglers to military bands.

In terms of customer care psychology these survey findings and future trends highlight some important lessons for airlines:

- Viewing a film on a plane is an isolated experience (using ear phones) which cuts passengers off from each other; it is also prone to frequent interruptions due to changing weather, flight deck announcements or fellow passengers moving around. Comedy is preferred because it usually requires less concentration than drama; it is easier to pick up the thread after an interruption. Furthermore, when people laugh together this creates a sense of camaraderie which reduces the isolation effect of the ear phones.
- The trend towards 'personalised' entertainment systems will enhance opportunities for time-layering by greatly reducing the chances of a passenger having previously seen the one selected film, thereby feeling that their time is being shaped for them rather than by themselves. This desire for personal time-shaping will be further catered for when passengers can take a break from whatever they are viewing and choose to eat, move around, or whatever, without missing out on 'their' film.
- Finally, the choice of over a hundred films will bring to flying a new opportunity for time-layering – the chronological time-zone. As the 100 films will range from 'golden classics' of the 1940s to films not yet released to cinemas, passengers will be able to move from the retro time-state to the future time-state as they wish.

9 The Customer Time-care Agency Business

9.1 INTRODUCTION

'Time agencies' have been in existence for many hundreds of years, but are now increasing rapidly in their nature and proliferation. Their purpose is to satisfy one or more of the following customer needs:

(a) To enable a customer to achieve an objective within less time than would otherwise be the case. (Time-compressing)
(b) To assist a customer in coping with fluctuating time pressures. (Time-smoothing)
(c) To undertake tasks which customers perceive as placing them in negative time-states. (Time-substituting)

9.2 TIME-COMPRESSING AGENCIES

Probably the oldest time-compressing agency is a brothel; it enables its clientele to achieve sexual satisfaction with minimal courtship and no on-going paternal commitments.

In a sense, a bank provides a similar *time-compressing* service; but there, of course, the similarity ends. By providing loans and paying interest on savings a bank enables its customers to achieve their economic objectives in less time than they would otherwise do. Banks are in fact involved in providing all three time-services. In addition to time-compressing, they provide short-term loans and overdrafts to help customers cope with short-term fluctuations in their financial affairs; this is time-smoothing. Finally, banks offer a range of money transmission services, direct debits and standing orders. These leave customers free to substitute positive time activities for the negative time which would otherwise need to be spent on paying bills, transporting money and other chores.

'Dating agencies' are also time-compressing; they have replaced the 'matchmaker' of earlier times by computer profile matching of customers seeking a relationship of some permanence. Despite the image of romance which they use to market their services, their key selling point is a sufficiently extensive data-bank which will accelerate the time-compressing process. On the basis of the old adage that 'time is money' dating agencies seek out profitable niches. Some will only deal with high earners (both male and female) and, on the basis that their affluent clients have more to gain financially from time-compressing, charge accordingly.

Other examples of time-compressing agencies are:

- Postal services, which are intended to transport letters and freight from one location to another quicker than the customer could.
- Courier services, which fill a need caused by inadequate postal services.
- Freight delivery services, which, like courier services, offer customers more efficient time-compressing than traditional postal services.
- Escort agencies, which offer companionship for a specified time without any time consuming preliminaries.

In the psychology of the customer, time-compressing agencies are judged, not simply by their efficiency in compressing time, but, where relationships are involved, in their effectiveness at reinforcing positive time-states. An undesirable companion, the contracting of a sexually transmitted disease, unanticipated surcharges, are all examples of ways in which the customer can be transposed from a positive to a negative time-state – with much reduced customer satisfaction.

9.3   TIME-SMOOTHING AGENCIES

Perhaps the most successful time-smoothing agency in the 1970s and up to the mid-1980s was 'Manpower'. This provided people with skills needed by companies to deal with peaking or unexpected demands. (Its troubles in the late 1980s were due to financial matters rather than its competence in time-smoothing.)

Manpower is but one of many thousands of temporary employment agencies providing the ubiquitous 'temp'. This type of agency will expand into new employment fields in the 1990s as individuals seek to shape their own time and as employers are more wary of taking on 'full-time' staff.

There are now temporary employment agencies for:

— Office jobs
— Production jobs
— Air crew
— Sea crew
— Doctors and nurses
— School teachers
— Executives
— Sales representatives
— Mercenaries
— Security staff
— Priests and Ministers

Typical of an agency for providing priests on a temporary basis (as distinct from temporary priests!) is Clerical Exchange International, based in Ireland. Its advertisement highlights a new niche for time-smoothing services: 'Have you ever thought of doing temporary supply for a priest in another part of the world? Do you experience difficulty getting cover for vacations/sick leave? we can help . . .'

When it comes to time-smoothing, the essential factors as far as the customer is concerned are competence, integrity and reliability. Temporary staff have to be at least as competent as their full-time colleagues. They must be sufficiently trustworthy to maintain confidentiality and comply with high ethical standards. They must be reliable in terms of working the hours contracted for, and of completing the contract period.

One danger which time-smoothing agencies need to avoid is that those people whom they send to a company do not create more demands on the time of supervisors and managers, thus negating their very purpose. In an increasingly volatile, unpredictable world it is safe to predict that the use of time-smoothing agencies will increase.

9.4 TIME-SUBSTITUTING AGENCIES

The future of time-substituting agencies is also bright as more women are in full-time employment outside the home. These agencies undertake tasks on behalf of the customer, and fall into three categories:

(1) Professional services
(2) Laborious services
(3) Chore services

Professional services are provided by those, such as accountants, solicitors and doctors, who have spent a significant time in acquiring their professional qualifications. It would be difficult for one individual to acquire the competence to be able to service himself on all matters of finance, law and medicine. Because time is finite for each one of us we can only qualify in one or two spheres by foregoing the chance to qualify in others. In other words, each individual foregoes the opportunity to use time to acquire proficiency in several spheres, in the knowledge that others will be competent to substitute for him in those areas.

Looking ahead with the narrowing of specialisation and increased access to knowledge through computerised data banks and television, it is likely that professional services will divide into 'paras' and 'niche specialists'. Paramedics, paralegals and para-accountants will be people who have attained a level of proficiency in their professional subject which will enable them to deal with most of a customer's needs for advice or action. 'Niche specialists' will be qualified in their profession, but will have concentrated on mastering in depth a narrow field of knowledge. The 'run of the mill' doctor, lawyer and accountant will disappear, overshadowed, if not crushed, by paras and niche specialists. Fees will continue to be charged to customers on a time basis, supplemented by a form of retainer which will give the client priority access to the profession required. (This retainer is, in effect, a time-compressing insurance.)

Laborious services are those which could be performed by the customer, but would impose heavy demands on physical energy and time. Digging a pit in which to install a swimming pool can be done by wielding a spade, but a mechanical digger will remove the physical burden from the customer as well as achieving the objective quicker. Many people prefer to substitute hours which are needed for home decorating with working hours which can finance hiring a painter and decorator. One threat to providers of laborious services is the invention of 'labour-saving devices'. These range from ironing machines to powered tools; from food processors to robotic lawnmowers.

A further threat is the invention of goods which obviate the need for any exertion. Self-cleaning ovens and self-defrosting refrigerators have long been on the market. Still to come are a wider range of non-iron clothing that looks as though it has been ironed, self-cleaning footwear that looks normal, and self-cleaning cars. Ultrasonic techniques will lead to self-dusting rooms; robotic bed-makers and garbage handlers are coming over the horizon.

Finally, there are chore services. Chores are usually performed in what for many people are negative time-states. There are some people, no doubt, who enjoy clearing blocked drains, cleaning lavatories, taking clothes to be mended, filling their cars with petrol, waiting in line to cash a cheque, buying postage stamps, tidying their children's rooms – but they are few and far between. There are, however, many people who are willing to perform these essential but boring tasks for a price. In the past they have worked as servants, in the future they will work as agents. 'Quotidien agencies', that is, those providing for recurring chores, will be one of the fastest growing segments in the service industry.

Bundling together a range of chores will be a competitive strategy. For example, an agency which promises to 'keep clean everything in the house' could be an attractive proposition for the career person. One problem would be gaining agreement on 'standards' of cleanliness. One person's clean home is another person's pigsty.

The trick will be to offer personalised chore services packages. This will require finding out from potential customers their least liked chores, then offering to service them on the basis of a fixed price, plus premium prices in relation to how important it is to the customer to find a substitute to undertake the chore. This is an example of customer care psychology pricing which focuses on the psychic value to the customer of the service, rather than the cost of the service incurred by the provider.

This type of customer psychology pricing has been used by the providers of professional services down the ages. In the 1990s it will be more commonly used by the providers of chore services.

9.5   CONCLUSION

Table 9.1 gives examples of the more common type of time-agencies. Hitherto their services fell into the three categories of:

(1) Time-compressing
(2) Time-smoothing
(3) Time-substitution

Looking ahead, competitive advantage will lie with those who are able to combine all three types of time. Perhaps the ultimate time-agency would be one that provided proxies to undertake social

Table 9.1 Examples of time agencies

Title	**Time-compressing agencies** Service being sold	What customer is buying
Advertising agencies	Marketing expertise.	Ability to make a positive impact on large numbers of potential customers within a short space of time.
Driving schools	Expertise in driving a car safely and in accordance with legal requirements.	Reducing the time needed to reach a state of proficiency required by law.
Estate agents	Data on accommodation for sale.	Reduce time needed to find a buyer for own accommodation or to purchase/rent accommodation.
Financial brokers	Knowledge of financial products and markets.	Speedy access to details of financial products and options.
Floral delivery	Guaranteed delivery of flowers to a specified location on a specified date.	Ability to make a social gesture with 'fresh' flowers despite distances involved.
Plant and heavy machinery hire	Equipment for undertaking physically demanding tasks.	Completing a physically and time-consuming task more quickly.
Pregnancy testing services	Expertise in diagnosing the existence or not of a fertilised ovum.	Reduces waiting time and enables earlier decision on a life-changing event.

continued on p. 150

Table 9.1   continued

Title	**Time-compressing agencies** *Service being sold*	*What customer is buying*
Slimming clubs	Expertise in losing weight through diet and other methods.	Ability to enhance self-image and improve health in a shorter time-span than if left to one's own devices.
Surveyors	Expertise in the structure of buildings.	Knowledge of possible structural defects which might otherwise only manifest themselves over a long time-span.
Ticket agencies	Entitlement of admission to an event for which tickets are required.	Assured admission in less time than it would take to purchase tickets at the location of the event.

Title	**Time-smoothing agencies** *Service being sold*	*What customer is buying*
Car hire	Use of a car for a specified period of time.	Ability to reduce travel time when own car is not available.
Dress hire	Use of articles of clothing for a specified period of time.	Ability to conform with dress appropriate to an event without spending a significant amount of time earning sufficient income for outright purchase. (This applies to all 'hire' agencies.)
Office services	Access to equipment and secretarial services.	Ability to use equipment and secretarial staff on an occasional basis and to cope with peaks in demand.
Kennelling	Safeguarding of pets in the absence of their owners.	Ability to keep commitments and respond to unexpected demands on one's time.

151

Title	Time-substituting agencies Service being sold	What customer is buying
Accountancy	Financial knowledge. Tax advice.	Substituting time spent on compiling accounts and tax returns. Reducing chances of spending negative time complying with regulatory requirements.
Addressing and circulatory services	Printing/writing addresses. Door to door delivery of circulars.	Substituting time spent on repetitive chores and walking.
Baby sitting	Guarding children while parents are absent.	Enables parents to spend more time in leisure time-zone or other zones.
Catering services	Preparation and serving of food. Temporary use of cooking and eating utensils.	Ability as host/hostess to spend more time with guests.
Chimney sweep	Expertise in evacuating dirt from chimneys.	Ability to substitute occasional chore with a more desired time-state. Avoidance of negative time-state due to injury.
Painters and decorators	Expertise in refurbishing premises.	Ability to substitute a time-consuming task with a more desired time-state.
Security services	Safeguarding of people, goods and premises.	Ability to substitute a time-consuming task with a more desired state; opportunity to substitute negative time-state of 'worry' with positive 'peace of mind'.

continued on p. 152

Table 9.1 continued

Title	Time-substituting agencies	
	Service being sold	*What customer is buying*
Valet services	Expertise in cleaning different types of equipment, particularly cars.	Ability to substitute an occasional time-consuming chore with a more desired time-state.
Window cleaners	Expertise in cleaning windows and other glass surfaces.	Ability to substitute a recurring chore with a more desired time-state.
Dog training	Expertise in modifying the behaviour of dogs.	Ability to substitute a time-consuming task with a more desired time-state.
Fencing services	Materials for enclosing an area; expertise in constructing fences.	Ability to substitute a time-consuming task with a more desired time-state.
Laundries	Cleaning and ironing of clothes.	Ability to substitute a recurring chore with a more desired time-state.
Maintenance services (all types)	Expertise in the maintenance and repair of equipment.	Ability to substitute a recurring time-consuming task with a more desired time-state. If on contract, removes need to spend time remembering to arrange for maintenance.
Office cleaners	Maintaining cleanliness and hygiene in offices.	Ability to substitute a recurring chore with a more desired time-state.

obligations which either clashed with other commitments or were too distant to attend, or were simply socially irksome. Proxy voters, proxy godparents, even proxy bridegrooms are acceptable in various parts of the world. Heads of state are 'represented' at various events by a proxy or an ambassador. Is it therefore too outlandish to visualise an 'ambassadorial service' whenever you wanted to be re-*present*-ed at some event? Such a service would be:

- Time-compressing, as it would greatly reduce travelling time.
- Time-smoothing, in that it would enable a number of social obligations to be undertaken at one time.
- Time-substituting, as it would enable you to select the most desirable event for personal attendance, or do your own thing.

Although intended as a humorous stimulant to thinking about the development of time-agencies, does not the seed of the idea rest in the phrase 'So and so asked to be remembered to you' – a case of a thwarted desire to be in two places at once?

10 The Life-style Time-zones

10.1 INTRODUCTION

A psychic time-zone is a continuum in which an individual experiences a variety of different time-states. Some experiences last milliseconds, others can go on for hours or days.

Our subconscious flits from zone to zone and, within any zone, from state to state. At any one point in time we are undergoing an 'experience' – time is passing in a particular way. Smells, sights or encounters can evoke a sense of time past. Anticipating events can propel us to an experience of the future. The trouble with the word 'anticipate' is that it is misused as a synonym for 'waiting', whereas its true meaning is to 'forestall'; to pre-empt a future experience. There is a world of difference between 'anticipating' one's marriage and 'waiting for it expectantly'.

Our minds are like a pinball machine, experiences being momentarily highlighted and then moving in an apparent random order from one psychic time-zone to another and from state to state. Clock time has different meanings for different people (see Table 10.1).

In this chapter we analyse a number of what are termed life-style zones, simply because their impact is more on the style of living of individuals rather than their standard of living. Therefore, as a generalisation life-style zones tend to have an indirect rather than direct impact on the development and evaluation of products and services.

The life-style zones are:

- Family
- Leisure
- Private
- Ritual
- Worship
- Work

Table 10.1 Customers' concepts of time

Clock time	Customers perception
Millennium – a thousand years	A symbol of continuing life. A time for reappraisal and renewal as one millennium ends and another begins.
Century – a hundred years	A time within which individual lives begin and end.
Decade – ten years	A period within which fashion and tastes undergo significant change.
Year – a measure of the time taken for the Earth to rotate round the Sun	A period for calculating interest on loans and savings. A period of guaranteed dependability of a car and most domestic appliances. The interval between increases in salaries. The period on which school fees are calculated. The period for a routine medical check. The period within which a vacation is planned. The period within which birthdays and anniversaries are celebrated. The period over which decoration and refurbishing takes place. The period in which taxes are calculated. The 'accepted' period for an engagement to last before marriage (Western societies). The 'accepted' period for not remarrying after death of spouse (Western societies).

continued on p. 156

156

Table 10.1 *continued*

Clock time	Customers perception
	The basic unit used for calculating an individual's entitlement to: Complete formal education Vote Marry Drive Smoke Consume alcohol Make financial commitment See different categories of films Sign contracts Undertake certain types of work Buy certain products.
Season – a quarter of a year	The period associated with traditional feasts and rituals. The period for purchasing/wearing certain types of clothes. The period for playing certain games. The period for consuming certain types of food and drink. The period for bestowing gifts and sending greeting cards. The period for launching certain products, e.g. fashion shows. The period for differential pricing.
Month – one twelfth of a year	The period within which salaries are paid. The period within which bills are due. The period on which a long holiday is based. The period on which certain magazines are published. The period determining the frequency of hairdressing (especially for men).

The period for determining the durability of certain clothes (particularly for babies).
The basis for calculating the rental for such goods as cars, television sets, telephones.
A common basis for calculating the price of season tickets on public transport.

Week – a quarter of a month

The period for purchasing provisions.
The period for calculating the length of a normal holiday.
The period for cleaning the car, cleaning shoes, cashing cheques and other chores.
The period for visiting a library.
The period for attending a place of worship regularly.
The period for defining the interval between episodes of television programmes.
The period for publishing news magazines.

Day – the period taken by the Moon to circumnavigate the Earth

The period between baths or showers.
The period for changing clothes.
The period within which three meals are eaten.
The basis for establishing fees and units of pay for work.
The period for which holidays are calculated.

10.2 FAMILY TIME-ZONE

Life-changing events influencing customers' perceptions in this psychic time-zone are:

— Weddings
— Births
— Divorce
— Death

Life-enhancing events include:

— Anniversaries
— Parties
— Graduations

Life-maintaining events range from visits to relations (which may sometimes be life-enhancing) to baby sitting or granny sitting.

Figure 10.1 lists both positive and negative time-states in the family time-zone. As far as customer care is concerned the important points to bear in mind are that the dominant psychological feelings are:

• Guilt
• Obligation
• Joy
• Fulfilment

Ways in which service providers can reduce 'guilt' are by offering opportunities for substitution and conspicuous atonement (e.g. an expensive present or overlarge greeting card). Guilt arises from perceived failure to abide by certain standards of behaviour. Increasingly, people feel guilty about spending insufficient time directly caring for the old old in their families. Those providing nursing and caring services for the old can help to reduce guilt through such means as:

(a) Providing a warm caring environment.
(b) Assisting the old to communicate with the family either by writing or regular telephone contact.
(c) Providing a range of daily activities which help the old to pass the time.

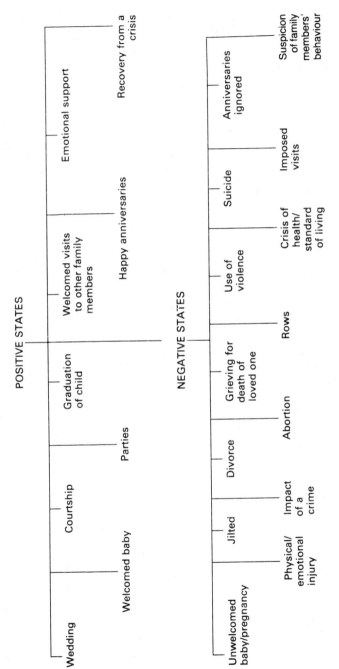

Figure 10.1 Family time-states

(d) Providing a range of medical and counselling services which would not be as accessible elsewhere.

By making available such services it is possible to provide an enhanced life-style for older people than they would otherwise be able to experience.

Obligation has its roots in tradition; reciprocal obligations abound in the family time-zone, be they annual visits, attending weddings or funerals, celebrating silver and golden wedding anniversaries. Services which can organise such events are a boon to customers while in this psychic time-zone. By coping with the chores such services as wedding organisers can enable people to discharge their obligations with minimal emotional expenditure, though the monetary expenditure may be high.

Joy and fulfilment are associated in the mind with such family events as weddings, births and graduations. Their negative twins, sadness and despair, also cast their dark shadow within the family time-zone. Counselling and advisory services which provide reinforcements of joy and fulfilment or the removal of sadness and despair are becoming more prominent and will grow enormously throughout the 1990s.

These life-style agencies may be state supported or private. They can be associated with established religion or with a 'new age' movement. The main point in terms of customer time-care is that their aim is to reinforce the positive time-states and reduce or remove the negative ones. For example, the negative time-state produced by a forgotten anniversary can be changed by an agency which ensures that flowers and a gift are delivered on the due date and that the forgetful spouse is reminded of the anniversary, privately, one day before the event.

While this may appear cynical it is surely no worse than the practice of some societies in European and African countries to hire 'professional mourners', thus reducing the negative time-state of grieving.

Medical and funeral services are involved in two psychic time-zones, biological and family. In the former their primary focus is on the physical aspects of living, in the latter their primary focus is on the emotional aspects of living. To optimise customer satisfaction it is necessary for doctors and undertakers to be aware of the specific zone in which they are operating. Failure to discriminate leads to impressions in the customers' minds of 'coldness' or 'inefficiency'.

The family time zone is a minefield for providers of services; it can be transformed into a gold-mine by recognising the various time-states which provide opportunities for Customer Time Care.

10.3 LEISURE TIME-ZONE

The key feature of the leisure time-zone is that it provides maximum opportunities for personal time-shaping. Customers enter this zone of their own free will and with expectations of 'doing their own thing'.

Leisure time is synonymous with 'free time' and 'own time'. It provides abundant opportunities for life-enhancement activities. Figure 10.2 illustrates the positive and negative states to be found in the leisure time-zone. Those who seek to profit from this zone would do well to concentrate on avoiding or eliminating the negative time-states. Their impact on customer care psychology can be significantly greater than those of the positive time-states. This is due to 'idealised envisioning' sometimes spurred on by exaggerated claims in advertising. By idealised envisioning I mean the tendency of people to envisage or 'dream about' a prospective pleasurable event be it a vacation, a trip to the theatre or a special night out. If reality does not meet the envisaged level of pleasure there is a sense of dissatisfaction. The greater the negative gap between the expected and the actual, the greater the disappointment. However, because individuals in the leisure time zone are anxious to experience the 'idealised situation' it takes only a very small enhancement of reality over that expected to produce greatly enhanced satisfaction.

The main time-concepts which service providers must guard against in the leisure time-zone are:

— Time-intrusions
— Time-disturbances
— Time-warps

Time-intrusions are activities from another psychic time-zone which reduce customer satisfaction. For example, advertisements in cinemas intrude into leisure time by distracting from the main leisure objective – enjoyment of a film. Market-researchers seeking opinions while a customer is enjoying a book is another example.

Time-disturbances are activities within the same psychic time-zone

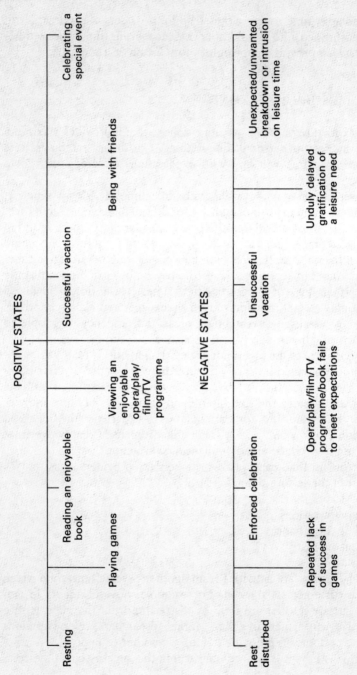

Figure 10.2 Leisure time-states

which reduce enjoyment. Fellow cinema goers talking is a common example which it may be difficult for cinema managers to control. However, the noise and smells of constant 'grazing' in a cinema is often the result of encouraged eating by cinema management.

Time-warps are sudden changes of psychic time-zone which are outside the control of an individual. The universal appeal of the film *Jaws* was that it highlighted the contrast between people enjoying themselves in the leisure time-zone and suddenly fighting off a killer shark. Less dramatic but if experienced in person, much less enjoyable, is suffering from a stomach upset while on vacation. Suddenly you move from the leisure to the biological time-zone.

It is because personal time-shaping is central to enjoying leisure that intrusions, disturbances and warps have a negative impact which are far more intense than the provider of a service may realise.

What's the fuss about? You had to wait an hour extra at the airport. Your hotel room wasn't ready on arrival. Ok there is some building going on near the pool, but you can't hear it for the music blaring out from those ghetto blasters. But you wanted two weeks in Turkey and we provided two weeks in Turkey. It's not our fault that you have a delicate stomach.

To sum up, customer satisfaction in the leisure time-zone requires:

- An assurance of personal time-shaping.
- An awareness of 'idealised envisioning'.
- An avoidance of intrusions, disturbances and warps.

10.4 PRIVATE TIME-ZONE

The essence of the private time-zone is the 'protection of personal space'. 'Space' in this context also means 'time'. Every individual needs to enjoy some degree of privacy, be it to perform bodily functions, express emotion, reflect, plan or simply ponder.

Personal stereos, televisions and telephones are examples of products designed primarily for the private time-zone. Perhaps the book is the oldest example of a personal product, though the claim may be contested by the chamber pot; in both cases they can only be used by one person at a time.

Figure 10.3 provides examples of positive and negative private

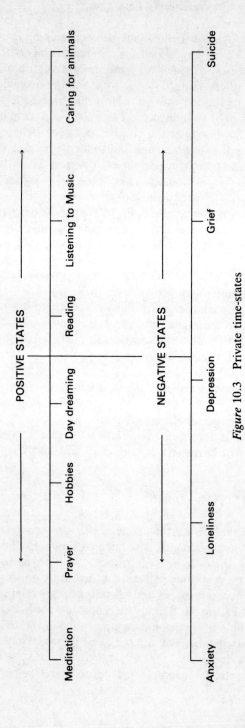

Figure 10.3   Private time-states

time-states. One disturbing trend is the use of drugs in the private time-zone to distort time. Time distortion is a unique characteristic of this zone. Drugs and alcohol can be used to make time temporarily more enjoyable, to elongate time by psychologically lengthening the span of an experience and finally to obliterate all sense of time at least temporarily – tragically, sometimes for ever. Suicide is the ultimate private act which ends time for the individual; its fatal attraction is that it generally shapes the time of others close to the individual. In this sense suicide is a manifestation of time power.

Those providing services in the private time-zone fall into four categories:

(a) Providers of pastimes such as crosswords and games which can be played alone not primarily for enjoyment, but to pass the time.
(b) Providers of personal advice from doctors to astrologers.
(c) Providers of individualised portions of food and drink.
(d) Providers of personal use products such as cassette players with earphones.

Looking ahead, there are four major growth areas of opportunity for products and services in the private time-zone:

(1) Foods for elegant 'grazing'. Eating on the hoof can be an un-edifying spectacle; however, as more people remain single and more partners are at work, 'grazing', which is a form of time-layering, will spread. As it gains social respectability, the packaging for ease of mobile eating and environmentally friendly disposal will become key marketing issues. One possibility is edible wrapping. It may sound revolutionary but it used to be the only means of consuming hand-held ice cream.
(2) 'Personal space suits'. Design on the principle of space suits worn by astronauts these will allow individuals to enjoy their personal space, cut off from noise, fumes and pickpockets. If carried to the ultimate, it would be possible while wearing the suits to perform basic bodily functions on the move, so to speak, disposing of the ordure at an appropriate time and space. However, even the most time-obsessed individual may balk at this opportunity to save fifteen minutes a day!
(3) 'Personal motor cars'. As individuals spend more time in their cars because of traffic jams and slower speed limits, motor manufacturers will provide, as an integral part of the vehicles, a

wide range of personal living aids designed for the customer's distinctive life-style.

(4) Somnolent activities. The most individualistic activity undertaken by human beings is sleep. Be it the length of time needed, preferred position, frequency of waking, tendency to snore, snoring pitch, or frequency and type of dreams, no two individuals are exactly alike.

Since we spend around a third of our life-time in some stage of sleep there is obvious scope for time-layering and time-compression. There are three major approaches being pursued to enable people to indulge in making fuller use of their sleeping time-state which bestrides both the biological and private time-zones:

(a) Hypnopedia;
(b) Cosmetic enhancement;
(c) Sleep control.

Hypnopedia, more commonly known as 'sleep learning', has been experimented with since the 1920s. Initiated at the US Naval School in Florida, it spread to Europe and has strong adherents in the USSR, France and Britain, where it was promoted by the British Sleep Learning Association. Even after seven decades there is inconclusive evidence of its efficacy. A major hurdle is that in a state of sleep the brain can only assimilate pictures; this rules out the use of language. However, experimenting continues with the prospect of a rich market for those who can guarantee an enjoyable sleep experience and/or one in which you can extend your knowledge.

Cosmetic enhancement: Putting on face lotions, curling hair or using a hairnet have been common activities through the ages. Unfortunately, the trade-off between night beauty preparation and the daytime results can be small or non-existent. Nevertheless, the desire to make fuller use of sleeping time is resulting in products which enable individuals to meet other needs whilst asleep. The gently massaging bed, a pillow which improves circulation of blood to the face, thus reducing the onset of wrinkles, deodorant pyjamas which reduce the need to spend time in the bath or shower are examples of time-layering products.

Sleep control: Chemicals to induce sleep or to keep people awake have long been around. They are slowly giving way to psychological methods. These range from sleep counselling to sleep clinics to help those who suffer from insomnia (inability to sleep) to hypersomnia (excessive sleep).

A market niche which is receiving greater attention is snorers, or more precisely the victims of snorers. Anti-snoring armlets, which give a slight shock to the snorer when the snore reaches a particular pitch, and special anti-snore pillows are two common examples of 'snore control' products. Men snore more than women, people snore more as they grow older; therefore as the life-span of the male lengthens there will be a growing market for anti-snore products.

Looking ahead, there is scope for an electronic service which wakes people up in the morning, gently, and with a 'message' appropriate to their usual 'waking-up mood'. For some, a specific type of music would be appropriate, for others an inspirational message or a humorous story might be more desirable. This service could be provided by a conference type telephone which does not need to be held to the ear, or by using an automatic cassette player to play tapes which are designed specifically to match the waking mood of the customer. The benefit of this approach would be that the individual wakes in a positive time-state.

It is in the private time-zone that individuals indulge their self-image. Increasing efforts will be made by providers of goods and services to probe the psyche and make available the requisites for a life-style which reinforces a positive self-image and/or compensates for a negative one.

Perhaps the greatest customer-time-care opportunity in the private time-zone will be 'pet care'. Products to ensure bouncing health, enhanced looks and protection from the elements will abound. Time-services such as exercising pets, transporting them, sheltering them and, in the end, disposing of them, will abound. Following the biological pattern of humans, as pets, particularly dogs and cats, live longer due to improved feeding, cossetting and veterinary services, there will be the emergence of the 'old old' pet and with it the growth of pet nursing homes where the owners can reassure themselves that their, by now incontinent and snapping, pets are having the time of their extended lives.

10.5   RITUAL TIME-ZONE

What differentiates this zone from all others is that while in it, the time of the individual is prescribed. Personal time-shaping is virtually impossible. Figure 10.4 illustrates positive and negative ritual time-states.

All events in the ritual time-zone are to some degree life-changing. Some rituals are relatively commonplace such as marriage, coming of age or funerals. Others such as receiving a knighthood, or becoming a Freeman of the City of London or a member of Rotary in Hicksville are restricted to a privileged few.

There are three major areas of customer care which draw life from the ritual time-zone:

(1) Professional and advisory services;
(2) Ritual apparel hire;
(3) Specialist caterers.

Professional and advisory services thrive on the ignorance of those exposed to ritual for the first time. A desire to present the right image, do the right thing, and avoid damage to self-esteem motivate people to seek out those for whom ritual is commonplace. Lawyers, priests, funeral directors, matchmakers are all masters and mistresses of ritual. Their income comes from knowing what is 'the done thing'.

Rituals tend to be one-off events as far as a particular individual is concerned. Participation in a ritual is usually signalled by wearing distinctive clothing. The expense of buying such apparel can be very high, therefore people prefer to hire it. This *ritual apparel hiring* extends to the more commonplace events of weddings and funerals. By wearing the prescribed apparel the individual feels at ease in the ritual time-zone. This also applies to quasi-rituals such as 'dressing up' for Royal Ascot races 'company dinners', and entertainment award ceremonies.

As well as prescribed dress, rituals often have prescribed foods and drink such as wedding cake, toasting the newly-weds with champagne, or particular dishes at barmitzvahs. *Specialist-caterers* in these fields have to be fully aware of the ritual involved and particularly of the need for pacing. Associated with such caterers can be professional 'masters of ceremony' who pace the serving of food, ensure that those who have a role are suitably briefed and that any order of precedence is followed correctly.

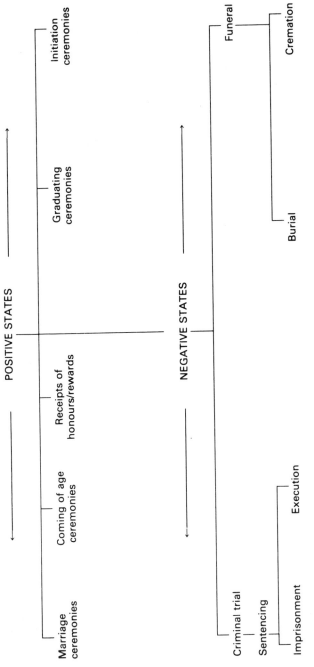

Figure 10.4   Ritual time-states

The ritual time-zone is peppered with 'common unique experiences'. Those who seek to provide services in this zone must always keep this in mind. Common unique experiences are weddings, award ceremonies and other situations which, although common to those organising them, are a unique experience to the individual involved for the first time.

10.6   SURVIVAL TIME-ZONE

The distinctive characteristic of the survival time-zone is that people would prefer not to enter it; once in it they want to get out – fast.

Figure 10.5 illustrates typical survival time-states. Providers of services in the survival time-zone are often government (state and local) services. Fire, ambulance, police and emergency medical care are examples of services designed to help people avoid getting into, or quickly getting out of, this zone.

Environmental awareness, a growing incidence of man-made catastrophes, and rising crime rates will stimulate demand for products and services relating to survival. Another impetus will be the increasing willingness of individuals to sue those suppliers whom they perceive as the cause of them being moved into the survival time-zone and/or loved ones perishing in it. The Channel ferry disaster at Zeebrugge, the Piper Alpha oil platform holocaust in the North Sea, the Hillsborough football stadium mayhem are all dramatic examples of people being suddenly thrust into the survival time-zone.

Day by day, car crashes, electrocutions, accidental poisoning and food poisoning can often be traced to faulty goods and services. Manufacturers and service providers will need to pay increasing attention to the implications of the survival time-zone. Clear instructions for use, anti-tampering packaging, repeated safety checks, more drilling of passengers in life-saving and emergency evacuation procedures will all be part of customer-time-care in the 1990s.

One growing shadow cast by the survival time-zone is claims for psychic hurt or damage. 'Hedonic damage' claims, so called because the source of the complaint prevents the plaintiff from enjoying life fully, will become commonplace. The concept behind these claims relates directly to customer-time-care. The disgruntled customer (or even someone close to the actual customer) is claiming that as a result of an event in the survival time-zone, their time has been distorted. Be it confinement to a wheelchair or recurring nightmares, or some

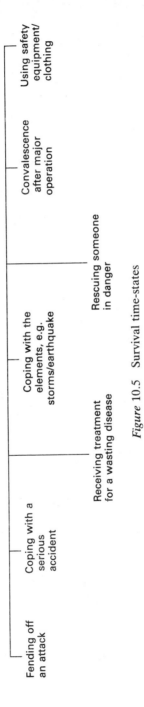

Figure 10.5 Survival time-states

other psychological or physical damage, the plaintiff is saying to the supplier of the guilty product or service, 'You have shaped my time in a way I did not want. You have reduced my opportunities for time-layering and time-compressing. You have denied me access to certain psychic time-zones and positive time-states. You have confined me to undesired zones and states. You have damaged my most precious possession – time.'

What chance does a manufacturer or service supplier have against such an entreaty?

Ensuring that all possible safety measures have been taken in the production and service delivery processes is no longer sufficient. Foreseeing and forestalling claims for hedonic damages are equally important in customer-time-care.

10.7   WAITING TIME-ZONE

The major feature of this zone in regard to customer-time-care is that the less time customers spend in it, the more satisfied they will be. Figure 10.6 lists examples of minor and major states.

Waiting is investing time in one zone to enable entry into another zone. We wait in line at the cinema in order to enter the leisure time-zone; we wait for the supermarket to open so we can enter the provisioning time-zone; we wait to check in at the airport so that we can enter the travel time-zone; we wait at the check-out at a supermarket so that we can leave the provisioning time-zone for another.

The main things which manufacturers and service providers need to keep in mind when dealing with customers in this zone are:

- Reduce waiting times to a minimum.
- Ensure that promised delivery times are kept or exceeded.
- Where a delivery time is likely to be delayed, give the earliest possible warning so that the customer can readjust his 'waiting clock'.
- For unforeseen delays provide regular and frequent up-dates on the causes of delay and give the *time* of the next announcement.
- Provide distractions, such as video presentations, for people in line; but make sure the cycle time does not lead to repetitive showings.
- Provide diversions such as meals, coach trips or films to help move the customer into another time-zone.

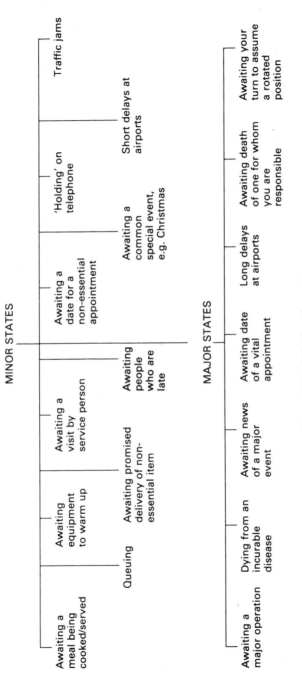

Figure 10.6 Waiting time-states

- Remember that 'waiting time' moves at different speeds. Generally, it is experienced as moving at a slower rate than clock time. One exception is while waiting or holding on the telephone, when the brain imagines time to have passed much quicker than the actual elapse of clock time; hence a two minute wait seems like a ten minute wait.

Waiting is usually perceived as a waste of time; the challenge for customer-time-care is to change that perception of waste either through time-compression or time-layering. Providers of services can, in this case, learn from the Japanese manufacturing technique of *Kanban*, or just-in-time.

Devised by Taiiti Ohno, a manufacturing executive in Toyota, *Kanban* (the Japanese word for 'sign') ensures that motor car parts are made only as needed and are then supplied to the next stage of production, literally, just in time. Using this computer-based technique, the waiting time for service in department stores, hotels, supermarkets, airlines and banks could be reduced. A *Kanban* approach to services would require:

— Encouragement to customers to place their orders early.
— Cross-training of staff who can be reassigned to areas of heaviest demand.
— Provision of desirable alternative time-zones to give opportunities for customers to satisfy other needs during the time required for delivery, so that they feel they are not 'waiting'.

10.8   WORSHIP TIME-ZONE

Some may wonder about the relevance to customer-time-care of the worship Time-Zone. It might be argued that worship is a continuing process for certain people. My purpose in including it is twofold:

— It is one of the sixteen time-zones which influences customer psychology.
— It provides an opportunity for extending customer-time-care.

Religion has a profound effect on customer needs and expectations. The Moslem abhorrence of alcohol and the Jewish aversion to pork are obvious examples. Holy places such as Mecca and

Lourdes have a marked impact on airlines. Religious festivals such as Christmas and Easter, Ramadan and Passover provide retailers with a significant amount of their annual turnover (see Figure 10.7).

In the 1990s, there are two opportunities for customer-time-care in this zone:

(1) The provision of a quiet place in airports, hypermarkets and railway stations for meditation and prayer.
(2) Offering a choice of religiously approved foods, not only in specialist restaurants but in hotels, on aircraft and even in fast food outlets.

Neither of these are new opportunities, but as the impact of the Moslem religion increases and the Judaeo-Christian religion declines, service providers will need to spend more time looking to Mecca if their prayers for increased business are to be answered.

10.9 CONCLUSION

Life-style time-zones are, by and large, where people prefer to spend their lives, exceptions being survival and waiting. The life-style zones provide the most opportunities for time-shaping, but less opportunities for time-compressing and time-layering. If you are enjoying being in a time-zone why bother to change it.

On the other hand, those who can assist customers to enhance or elongate their time in the positive time-states of life-style zones will reap rich rewards. People want to get all they can out of their chosen life-style.

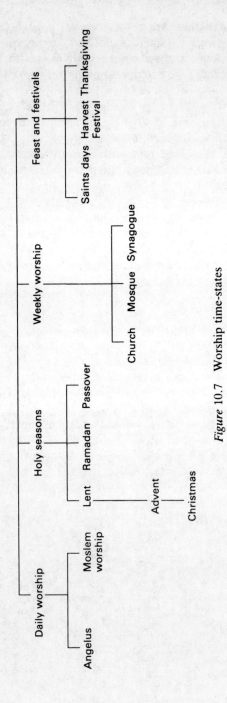

Figure 10.7 Worship time-states

11 The Life-work Time-zones

11.1 INTRODUCTION

Much of our lives are preoccupied with earning the money to enable us to enjoy a particular life-style.

Travelling, working, provisioning and communicating all have to be done, to some degree, by every individual. In this chapter we shall consider these four major psychic time-zones. We shall look at opportunities which can exist to enhance customer-time-care in each of the zones.

Whether we are acting as providers of services or customers, we need to be aware of the factors which shape perception in relation to customer-time-care. As will be seen in Table 11.1, there are both conscious and subconscious perception shapers at work moulding the customer's judgement of satisfaction.

We shall begin by considering the travel time-zone and then proceed to the zones of work, provisioning and communicating.

11.2 TRAVEL TIME-ZONE

The soldiers of Julius Caesar and the soldiers of Napoleon travelled at the same speed. For many thousands of years the speed of man was limited by one factor – the endurance of the horse. The first break-through in enhancing the speed of travel occurred not on the ground, but in the air. Ballooning, devised in France, permitted man to cover greater distances at a faster rate than ever before; unfortunately, the balloon failed to take off, so to speak, as a form of travel, because of its small pay-load, its vulnerability and the unpredictability of its eventual landing place.

The allure of the balloon was put in the shade by the first passenger steam train in 1825. The train ushered in, not simply a new age of travel, but a new concept of time. Suddenly, the unit of time for estimating the arrival of travellers moved from the day or hour to the minute. As we have seen, clock time had to be more accurate than before; synchronising of time became necessary between towns and,

Table 11.1 Customer-time-care – perception shapers

Industry	Conscious perception shapers	Subconscious perception shapers
Airlines	Route network	Opportunities to reach destination more quickly.
	Punctuality	Assurance of meeting deadlines, keeping appointments.
	Cabin crew	Assistance in time-layering.
	Comfort	Enhanced opportunities for time-layering.
	Added value features like free chauffeured cars	Opportunity for time-compressing especially in a new location.
	Food and wine	Time-layering on long-haul; time-compressing on short-haul.
	Smooth transfers	Time-compressing; reduced waiting time.
	Separate lounges	Permits time-layering and provides opportunities for private time.
Airports	Good baggage handling	Time-compressing; reduction in waiting time.
	Lack of congestion in public areas	Reduced waiting time; opportunities for time-layering.
	Swift speed of check-in	Time-compressing.
	Well stocked duty free shop	Opportunity for time-layering in the family and provisioning time-zones.
	Swift transport to city	Time-compressing.
	Clear signage	Time-compressing.

Hotels	High quality service	Positive time-states in appropriate zones will predominate.
	Standard of room	Opportunities for effectiveness in both the leisure and work time-zones.
	Ambience	Reinforces positive time-states.
	Central location	Time-compressing with ready access to locations for work and leisure.
	Cuisine	Assurance of positive time-states in the biological time-zone.
	Exercise gym	Opportunities for positive time-states in the biological and leisure time-zones.
Car rental	Availability of requested model	Time-compressing because of reduced 'learning' time.
	Reliability	Absence of time-distortions.
	Speed of collecting car	Time-compressing.
	Choice of car	Opportunity to indulge in retro-time or forward time, depending on the model.
	Back-up and emergency services	Reassurance of help if in survival time-zone.

later, countries; standard time-zones came into existence in the United States.

In the mid-nineteenth century the discovery of oil in North America stimulated the use of that fuel in place of steam. This, in turn, led in 1885 to the invention of the first motor car powered by an internal combustion engine. Another new age dawned, with the drastic reduction of time needed to travel by road from one location to another. (Ironically, the coming of the car heralded the beginning of the end of the ozone layer as the rubber trees of the Amazonian jungle were depleted to make tyres; but that's another big story.)

In 1888, the pneumatic tyre was invented resulting in the modern bicycle; this became the most affordable form of travel for the majority of mankind and so it remains.

Towards the end of the nineteenth century came a plethora of public transport vehicles; the omnibus, the tram and the underground railway. The twentieth century had hardly dawned when there came the prospect of the next transport revolution with the invention of the aircraft. Its impact is discussed later in this chapter.

11.3 DISTINCTIVE CHARACTERISTICS OF THE TRAVEL TIME-ZONE

Although it is often at a subconscious level, the primary requirement of customers while in the travel time-zone is safety. A conflicting but dominant need is speed. Day in and day out car drivers trade off safety against speed and find they have arrived in the survival zone rather than their planned destination.

Providers of transport services have many of their activities prescribed by law. This is to protect their passengers. Unfortunately, because they fear that the mention of safety could have an adverse effect on their passengers, operators do not communicate to passengers the true reasons for delays.

Figure 11.1 provides a resumé of positive and negative travel time-states. Reducing or eliminating the negative states is more likely to enhance customer satisfaction than reinforcing the positive time-states. Arriving at a destination ten minutes behind schedule is perceived by passengers as poor performance; arriving ten minutes before schedule is perceived as a freak occurrence or poor scheduling.

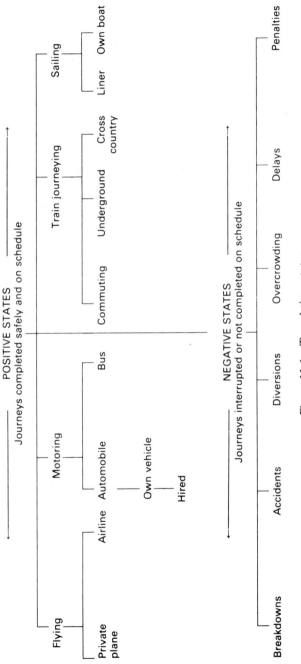

Figure 11.1 Travel time-states

11.4   CARING FOR NEGATIVE TRAVEL TIME-STATES

Negative travel time-states have their roots in one or more of the following:

(a) Breakdowns
(b) Accidents
(c) Diversions
(d) Overcrowding
(e) Delays
(f) Penalties

All modes of transport are man/robot made and are prone to breakdown. Any breakdown is a time-distortion, requiring rescheduling of time-plans and a move into an undesired time-zone such as waiting or survival.
Avoiding breakdowns calls for:

— Higher quality components;
— Improved breakdown warning systems;
— Simple replacement of broken parts;
— Speedy substitution by another vehicle;
— Training of drivers (of all types) to avoid damaging habits; and to anticipate likely breakdowns.

Accidents are a more acute form of time-distortion than breakdowns. They can result in time-warps whereby the victim is not only catapulted physically but also psychically into the survival zone.
Accidents due to vehicle faults require the same treatment as for breakdowns. Where accidents are due to human error or result in injury or death, any service provider involved needs to be capable of dealing with both the physical and psychic impact. Particular attention needs to be paid to:

• Encouraging passengers to pay attention to safety procedures.
• Where appropriate, ensuring that safety drills are regularly practised by all concerned.
• Training staff in both basic physical and psychic rescue routines.
• Having effective communications procedures to keep informed all those involved in or directly affected by the accident.

Diversions, in the sense of rerouting, are another source of time distortion. Adding to journey time and therefore interfering with planned schedules, they prevent the passenger from entering the desired time-zone as planned. Where a service provider is involved in the diversion, the aim should be to enable passengers to contact their destination either directly or through the service provider. Being reassured that the other party is aware of the delay reduces the anxiety of the customer and can even give 'permission' to move into another time-zone.

Overcrowding on public transport is the result of mismatching supply and demand. In relation to customer-time-care, overcrowding is not only uncomfortable but it has adverse time-effects:

— It inhibits time-layering such as reading or knitting while travelling.
— It can cause time distortion particularly if the traveller is also in the leisure or work time-zones. In the leisure zone the inadequate personal space makes relaxation difficult; in the work zone, confidential discussions with a colleague cannot take place.

Varying prices and incentives to travel off peak are traditional devices which public transport providers employ to smooth out supply and demand. Some psychological devices which might make unavoidable overcrowding more tolerable are:

• Release of aromas in underground or train compartments or aircraft to give a sense of fresh air or even induce a slight soporific effect of limited duration.
• Use of sound reduction technology which cancels the noise of the vehicle by matching it with an anti-noise wave which is 180 degrees out of phase with the original noise wave.
• Providing 'recuperating rooms' for use by passengers after a journey as distinct from 'waiting rooms' before embarking on a journey. Such rooms would be accessible for one hour after the arrival of a train or plane, by use of a special encoded ticket.

It is interesting to note that in Singapore time is used as a control mechanism on the underground railway. Tickets are valid for only thirty minutes; when time expires there is a penalty to pay.

Penalties for infringing rules governing the validity of tickets and other infringements of company regulations produce a negative time-state, particularly in the genuinely ignorant passenger. This problem will increase as ticket controls become more automated. Unfortunately, many of the infringements will be intentional. The best recourse open to the service provider is to simplify fare structures and spend more time explaining the rules to passengers.

The travel time-zone is the one in which humankind can compress time and space most effectively. It is also the one in which there is the greatest vulnerability to the forces of nature and the follies of man. Lives are lost because of tempests and storms; even more lives are lost because of careless or drunken driving.

The challenge for those who produce and provide the means of travel is to help humankind protect itself from itself. Travellers live with the threat of the semtex bomb in the cabin of an aircraft and the drunken killer at the wheel of the car. Advances are being made in the detection of bombs and weapons at airports. Cars are being fitted with fail-safe alcohol braking mechanisms which all drivers must breathe into and which will only release the brake when there is no or little trace of alcohol. The travel time-zone is becoming ever more crowded on earth and the next step will be mass transit in space.

There follows a customer-time-care analysis of airlines. The methodology outlined can be adapted for other industries and other time-zones.

11.5   A CUSTOMER-TIME-CARE ANALYSIS OF AIRLINES

The first aircraft flew in 1903. It was then in the psychic time-zone of Leisure – a hobby for the adventurous. After the First World War when it became a weapon of war, it moved into the psychic time-zone of communications; a means of speeding up mail delivery, particularly across the USA.

Only in the 1930s did it move into the psychic zone of travel time as aircraft became capable of carrying more than two passengers. They also became faster and safer. Airlines began to come into operation in the 1930s and reduced travel time across America and the empires of Great Britain and Holland.

It was not until the 1960s that airlines became providers of mass transportation; the jet plus the development of wide-bodied aircraft brought airlines into a major service industry whose impact has shaped other industries such as travel agents, hotels, car hire, catering and airports.

Few, if any, service industries impinge on so many psychic time-zones and provide opportunities to care for a variety of time-states. In the 1980s, they have been pioneers of customer care programmes. But these have not been wholly successful since such programmes paid insufficient attention to the psychic time dimensions of their customers. As will be shown below these dimensions, properly analysed and managed, will bring airlines rich rewards.

11.5.1 Dominant Time-zone

Travel. Most passengers use airlines because they want to complete a journey of at least one hundred miles as swiftly as possible. Journeys of less than one hundred miles are likely to be undertaken by alternative means of travel. However, travel by air over short distances comes into play where:

— The terrain is rugged or without proper roads.
— An area of water has to be crossed.
— The life of an individual is at stake.

The distance covered by aircraft tends to be measured in time units of hours and minutes rather than miles or kilometres. Passengers talk of a 'three hour flight' or a 'fifty minute flight'. Even when journey time exceeds a day – for example, flying from Stockholm to Auckland – the flight is measured in hours and not days. What the customer is seeking is a reduction in travel time compared with other modes of transport. What customers are buying is travel time, but they are, in the 1990s, seeking satisfaction for other time needs.

11.5.2 Related Time-zones

Global Time

More than any other service industry, with the exception of banking and financial services, airlines need to be sensitive to global time. Operating 365 days a year (366 in a leap year) twenty-four hours per day and crossing global time-zones within and between countries, airlines are at the mercy of the clock. Customers seek departure and arrival times which are congruent with their work and leisure needs. Concorde provided man with the first opportunity to 'reverse' clock time. Businessmen leaving London at 8 a.m. local time can arrive in

New York at 7 a.m. Similarly, Concorde can make it feasible to leave London at 4 a.m. and arrive in New York at 3 a.m. There would be a further time advantage since journeys by road to London Heathrow and from Kennedy Airport would be far quicker during the night than early in the morning. However, businessmen, other than insomniacs, are unlikely to be attracted by this scheduling.

The global time which permits time reversal on the east–west journey across the Atlantic does not work in reverse. Leaving New York at 7 p.m. local time will result in an arrival time in London of approximately 3 a.m. As a consequence business passengers flying out to New York by Concorde purchase three seats in Economy Class on a Jumbo leaving New York at 10 p.m. The cost of those three seats is similar to the cost of one Concorde seat. Lying asleep across the three seats the customer arrives in London at 7 a.m. refreshed and ready for a day's work.

This sequence offers opportunities for a Concorde out–Jumbo sleeper back, time package.

Biological Time

Air travel affects body mechanisms which can lead to discomfiture and illness. While flying across global time-zones it is easier to adjust your watch than your metabolism. On a journey to Tokyo your watch may register that it is 7 a.m., whereas for your body it is 10 p.m. – a difficult time to enjoy breakfast. Equally, on a return journey from Tokyo to London, you could find yourself eating three breakfasts.

Planning the timing and type of food and drink to be provided in a manner congruent with the biological needs of passengers will give an airline competitive advantage. It is feasible to imagine airlines offering a harmless but effective 'time pill' which puts passengers to sleep for the duration of the journey. The drawback to such an arrangement would be the problem of waking up the passenger for take-off and landing, not to mention emergencies. On the other hand, the provision of automatic self-correcting safety belts and the use of code words or sounds to bring passengers out of a type of hypnotic sleep could provide an opportunity for customer care leadership.

Work Time

Airlines are focusing on this psychic time-zone to attract business customers; the provision of PCs, cellular phones and secretarial assistance is becoming commonplace. The problem is how to segregate the assiduous workaholic from the maudling alcoholic. Furthermore, how can the working passenger be sheltered from the regular offerings of food, drink, duty free goods and films which are the 'goodies' associated with flying First Class or Business Class. One approach would be to offer relatively spartan service, guaranteed segregation in a work-booth and the 'time displacement' device of a super meal for two when the air journey is over.

Leisure Time

For many the air journey is the means to and from a holiday. There can therefore be advantages in using the device of elongating time by integrating the journey into the holiday. Currently, it is left to the passenger to use this device, often resulting in intoxication ('What else is there to do?'). Airlines usually provide 'fun packs' for children, so why not 'fun packs' for adults?

Survival Time

Passengers perceive flying as dangerous. There is a need to ensure that they are well aware of safety drills. Use should be made of videos both at waiting points and on the aircraft to provide or back up instructions on safety procedures.

Provisioning Time

Airlines have recognised that there is profit in selling duty free goods. In recent years this has extended to mail order for luxury items. Many such items are impluse buys. When ordered by mail, the time-lapse can cause second thoughts in the mind of the customer. Truncating the purchase period will enhance customer satisfaction; this might be done by having stocks of goods at all points of arrival. Passengers ordering goods on the outward journey could then collect them on arrival or on return to the original point of departure.

Communications Time

This is a new and expanding field which will appeal to the business passenger able to maintain telephone and facsimile contact throughout a flight. However, the technological advantages may be offset by disturbances to passengers in other psychic time-zones. Interruptions to meals, films and sleep as fellow passengers are 'plugged in'; efforts to re-establish disconnected calls; reactions to 'bad news', all have to be kept in mind when planning how best to take advantage of this customer time care opportunity.

Waiting Time

This is a negative time-zone which airlines must keep to the minimum if they are to secure a reputation for customer care. As far as airlines are concerned there are various types of waiting:

— Accident prevention waiting – when repairs or replacement of parts is necessary.
— Systems breakdown waiting – when one or more components of the various support systems fails, for example, computer reservations.
— Imposed waiting – when some authority, such as air traffic control, imposes a delay.
— Crew induced waiting – when a crew member fails to appear or else performs incompetently.
— Passenger induced waiting – when a passenger fails to appear after checking-in, or for medical or other reasons, delays take off.

The psychic impact of waiting time can be reduced by diversions and regular reliable communications.

Opportunities for Time-layering: On top of travel time the airline can layer:

- Biological time — provision of food and drink; availability of toilets and hygiene aids.
- Work time — provision of business equipment and air-to-ground communications.
- Leisure time — provision of visual and audio communications; fun packs; visits to the cock-pit.
- Provision time — opportunity to buy presents and duty-free goods.

Opportunities for Truncating Travel Time: Speed up check-in and baggage retrieval; have taxis as well as hire cars available and fully briefed taxi drivers on arrival; have hotel booking data completed on the aircraft.

Opportunities for Elongating Time: Minimal interruptions to those wanting to work or sleep; make journey part of holiday from time of check-in.

Potential Time-warp: Emergency which moves customer from travel psychic time-zone to survival psychic time-zone.

Critical Points on Core Time: Remember that passengers perceive the journey as from door to door, not airport to airport. Better to extend estimated time of arrival to give impression of arriving early.

Critical Points on Peripheral Time: On a short journey the peripheral time, i.e. getting to and from the airport, checking in, waiting at gate, collecting baggage, can be equal to or longer than the core time. Peripheral time on air journeys is negative time. Need to provide diversions and be seen to care for customers on the ground as well as in the air. Why not use retired staff as ground carers?

11.6 WORK TIME-ZONE

The distinctive characteristic of the work psychic time-zone is that it is structured and is perceived as having a clear beginning (first job) and end (retirement).

From the standpoint of customer-time-care the role of service Providers is to:

— Assist individuals to meet their work-related goals.
— Reduce the physical and psychic demands of work.
— Enable the development of individual potential.
— Enhance and extend opportunities for wealth creation.

11.7 WORK SERVICES AND PRODUCTS

Figure 11.2 provides an insight into different work time-states. There is a plethora of products and services available to reinforce the positive and reduce the negative states. Examples of these are:

(a) Suppliers of finance;
(b) Suppliers of raw materials;

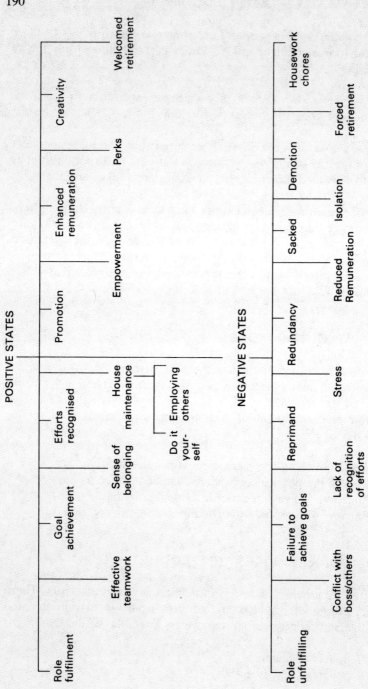

Figure 11.2 Work time-states

(c) Suppliers of data;
(d) Suppliers of equipment;
(e) Suppliers of techniques;
(f) Suppliers of advisory services;
(g) Suppliers of security services.

Banks and financial institutions are suppliers of finance. In terms of customer-time-care, banks are in the time-compression business. They provide loans which enable work goals to be achieved in a shorter time than would be possible if they were self-financing. They enable people to accumulate wealth more quickly by paying interest on savings. Money has been described as 'information in motion'; banks provide the means to transfer money across the globe in terms of milliseconds, enabling a customer to gain competitive advantage.

Just as banks feed the financial needs of commerce and industry, suppliers of raw materials feed its needs for means of manufacturing goods. In recent years, suppliers of fuels, minerals, wood and food have been forced to operate not only in the work psychic time-zone but also in the chronological and biological zones. Mines need to be landscaped, oil spillages must be cleared, trees have to be replaced, and food has to be protected from dangerous chemicals.

Suppliers of data have expanded tremendously with advances in telecommunications; they therefore operate in the communications psychic time-zone as well as the work zone. Essentially, they are in the time-compressing business making it possible to reach decisions more swiftly.

Suppliers of equipment are also in the time-compressing business, making it feasible to perform specific operations much more quickly than if only human power was used. Some will also be in the time-layering business making products which perform a number of operations simultaneously, and/or producing a range of products from one source. We shall shortly return to considering the 'time element' in a wide range of products and services.

Suppliers of techniques are in the time-compressing business; in many cases they will also be in the avoidance of time-distortion business. Many techniques are devised to reduce error, avoid breakdowns and accidents, forewarn of danger and correct mishaps. By these means the suppliers of techniques can help to reduce the changes whereby customers move into negative time-states at work.

Suppliers of advisory services have a similar role. In broad terms they can be divided into two types:

(1) Pro-active advice on business opportunities and plans.
(2) Reactive advice on coping with the failure of business plans.

Pro-active advisers focus on helping clients to stay in positive time-states. Strategic consultants, executive searchers, venture financiers and, in some cases, merchant bankers are typical pro-active advisers. Reactive advisers aim to help reduce the impact of negative time-states. Administrators, receivers, liquidators, outplacement consultants and, in some cases, merchant bankers are typical re-active advisers.

Critical to the success of the efforts of any adviser is to identify the time-state within which the client is working; be aware of related time-states and other relevant psychic time-zones; be able to empathise with the client and help make a smooth transition from one state or zone to another.

Suppliers of security services range from doormen to night watchmen, from special couriers to patent agents. What links them is the safe-keeping of the resources and integrity of the company. They are essentially preventers of time-distortions resulting from arson, theft or breaches of regulations. The chances of such distortions will increase as government agencies and bodies such as the European Commission issue more and more regulations. In common parlance, the role of such suppliers of security services, as compliance officers, is to spend their time ensuring that company officials do not end up 'doing time'.

11.8   TIME PRODUCTS AND SERVICES

The work psychic time-zone produces an enormous variety of products and services. All of these in some way carry a time connotation. Table 11.2 lists examples. An explanatory word on the categorisation and a comment on some of the products and services will put the time connotation into perspective.

Products and services can be categorised as:

— Time-recurring
— Life-time extending
— Time-compressing
— Time- displacing
— Time-conforming
— Time-enhancing

Table 11.2   Types of time products and services

Time-recurring activities

Products	*Services*
Washing machines	Office cleaning
Dish washers	Gas supplies
Vacuum cleaners	Electricity supplies
Cookers	Fast food
Food and drink	Supermarkets
Water	Office bureaux
Basic clothing	Banks
Newspapers and magazines	Post offices
	Public toilets
	Water companies
	Newsagents

Life-time extending

Products	*Services*
Lifts	Medical
Power tools	Dry cleaning
Cosmetics	Hairdressing
Gymnasiums	Health care
Refrigerators	
Freezers	

Time-compressing

Products	*Services*
Cars	Garages
Aircraft	Airlines
Trains	Airports
Bicycles	Travel agents
Motor cycles	Stations
Microwave ovens	Car hire
Prepared foods	Railways
Food processors	Computer maintenance services
Computers	Software development
Bank loans	Banking

Time-displacing

Products	*Services*
Telephone	Telecommunications
Radio	Radio/TV guides

---

continued on p. 194

Table 11.2   *continued*

Television	Video rental
Answering machines	Answering services
Video recorders	

Time-conforming

Products	*Services*
Uniforms	Funeral undertaking
Formal wear	Wedding/banquets organising
Jewellery for special events	Honeymoon resorts
Special care hire	

Time-enhancing

Products	*Services*
Luxury goods	Boutiques
Expensive clothes	Couturiers
Expensive food and wine	Grand hotels/Restaurants
Vacation	Resort hotels
Ocean liners	Travel agents
Paintings and objets d'art	Cruises
Books	Museums and galleries
Sports equipment	Booksellers
Saving and investing products	Specialist sellers
Films	Banks and financial institutions
Plays	Cinemas
Games	Theatres
	Stadiums
	Swimming pools
	Golf courses
Videos	Video rental
Health foods	Health farms
Wines	Wine merchants

11.9   TIME-RECURRING PRODUCTS AND SERVICES

Throughout our lives there are some activities which have to be undertaken at regular intervals; monthly, weekly, daily, as the case may be. Examples of these activities are eating, sleeping, personal hygiene, keeping up to date with the news, and housework.

All such activities are life-maintaining, many of them are chores. The attraction of time-recurring products and services to the customer is that they reduce or remove the chore element. This is obvious in consumer durables such as washing machines; less obvious is the practice of newspapers to provide a summary of the news on the front page, allowing the reader to reduce the time taken to keep updated on events occurring in all time-zones.

As people seek to avoid the negative time-states associated with chores, 'quotidien services' will grow apace. One interesting change in Western societies is the replacement of manpower by automation in carrying out 'dirty jobs'. Garbage collection, clearing drains and disposing of sewage are examples of activities which until the 1960s had low social status and even lower pay. In the 1990s, customers are willing to pay higher premiums for these types of service. The old adage, 'Where there's muck there's brass' needs updating to 'Where there's muck there's gold'.

11.10 LIFE-TIME-EXTENDING PRODUCTS AND SERVICES

Without lifts there would be no skyscrapers. Without medical services there would be more corpses. Without dry cleaning there would be more expenditure on clothes and furnishings. Without power tools there would be more deaths from heart strain. Without cosmetics there would be . . . fewer disillusioned partners the morning after?

This category of time-products and services relates primarily to life-enhancement needs, though some, such as medical services, are also involved in satisfying life-change needs. What they have in common is that they are perceived by customers as helping them to enjoy positive time-states in the biological psychic time-zone.

Lifts, for example, save energy which would otherwise be expended on climbing a fifty-storey building and then descending. Lifts are also time-compressing since they greatly reduce vertical travel time. Similarly, power tools are perceived by customers as saving energy and time in a negative state in the work psychic time-zone. Refrigerators and freezers not only extend the edible time-span of food, they reduce the need to spend time in the provisioning psychic time-zone.

These examples provide a clue to manufacturers and service providers of how to gain competitive advantage by the device of 'time-plexing'. The more psychic time-zones in which a product or service can operate, the more it will appeal to customers. Thus 'time-duplexing' would describe a product or service which provides satisfaction to customers in two psychic time-zones; 'time-triplexing' involves three psychic time-zones, and so on, to 'time-deciplexing' for ten psychic time-zones – a theoretical rather than a realisable concept at this stage.

11.11   TIME-PLEXING

Time-plexing differs from time-layering. The former describes a product or service which can be used simultaneously by customers in different psychic time-zones. For example, customers in a hotel could be seeking satisfaction in such zones as:

- Biological – having a quick snack.
- Work – holding a conference.
- Leisure – vacationing.
- Travel – stopping en-route for a rest.
- Family – holding a wedding reception.

The customers in each psychic time-zone will use different criteria in judging the quality of the services the hotel provides. In each psychic time-zone they need a different type of customer-time-care.

Time-layering, on the other hand, is the process of enabling a customer to operate in more than one psychic time-zone simultaneously.

It is important to bear this difference in mind as we continue to consider other types of time products and services.

11.12   TIME-COMPRESSING PRODUCTS AND SERVICES

These products and services enable customers to achieve satisfaction of their needs in a shorter time than would otherwise be possible.

Many of the products and services relate to travel, but food preparation, which can be a chore, has been transformed by the invention of microwave ovens, food processors and prepared foods.

11.13   TIME-DISPLACING PRODUCTS AND SERVICES

'Time-displacing' occurs when a customer is able to enjoy an experience which occurs at a different point in global time from that at which the experience took place. A transatlantic telephone call enables two people to talk to each other although both are talking at a different time of day. Similarly, radio and television enable people to share concurrently an experience which is occurring at different points in global time throughout the world.

Perhaps the two most effective time-displacement products are the telephone answering machine and the video recorder. The popularity of the answering machine is that it enables an individual to receive telephone messages while being elsewhere. It also allows time-compressing since, although a significant interval may have lapsed between the receipt of each message, they are played back consecutively without any intervals. A day's calls can be received in minutes.

The video recorder can enable a customer to shift days at the press of a button, enjoying an experience at a different time from when it originally occurred. Saturday night's viewing can be changed to Wednesday. Time contraflowing can be indulged in by instant play back, an experience can be 'frozen' in time. The video allows people to indulge in time-shaping; to be in two places at once. One of the great fears of humankind is the fear of missing something. People seek to have their time-cake and eat it; sophisticated televisions which enable the viewer to check other channels by means of a small inset on the TV screen, without missing what they are viewing, is the answer to this aspiration.

11.14 TIME-ENHANCING PRODUCTS AND SERVICES

All these products and services aim to give the customer a 'good time'. They are aimed at embellishing social status, building positive self-esteem and making life a bit brighter.

The dilemma for those who manufacture such goods or provide such services is that they need to attract customers by creating high expectations, which then need to be at least satisfied and preferably exceeded. Establishing a positive imbalance between promise and delivery is the major challenge.

More than with any other type of time products, a key element of enhancement is providing psychic added-value. A phenomenon of the 1990s will be 'inconspicuous consumption'. Providers of luxury will need to expend greater efforts in providing intrinsic value rather than extrinsic wealth. Enabling customers to shape their time in a way that ensures an optimising of positive time-states will be the biggest luxury of all.

11.15   PROVISIONING TIME-ZONE

In the beginning God provided Adam and Eve with every physical thing they needed; but they disobeyed God's rule and as a result were punished. Throughout the ages that punishment has passed from generation to generation – it is called shopping.

There are in truth both positive and negative provisioning time-states as shown in Figure 11.3. In this chapter, we shall focus on the customer psychology of routine shopping, rather than shopping for gifts or luxuries. In the modern world, most shopping takes place in three locations:

(1) Supermarkets
(2) Department stores
(3) Home shopping

11.16   SUPERMARKETS

The modern supermarket is the result of responding to customer needs for time-compression. Whereas until the late 1950s routine provisioning required visits to a number of specialist stores, the supermarket provides a wide range of goods under one roof. By combining the payment for goods to one point of time and location – the check-out – the time required for a variety of transactions is compressed into one.

Three time-sensitive innovations have accelerated the growth of supermarkets:

(1) The car makes possible one journey in place of many for transporting goods in quantity.
(2) The freezer makes it possible to reduce the frequency of journeys by safeguarding the durability and quality of foods which would otherwise perish.
(3) The computer has helped speed up inventory control and price calculations. This reduces the chances of additional visits for out-of-stock items and speeds the flow of customers at check-outs.

Supermarkets have given a great deal of attention to customer psychology in recent years and have designed their stores and displays on the basis of such findings as:

199

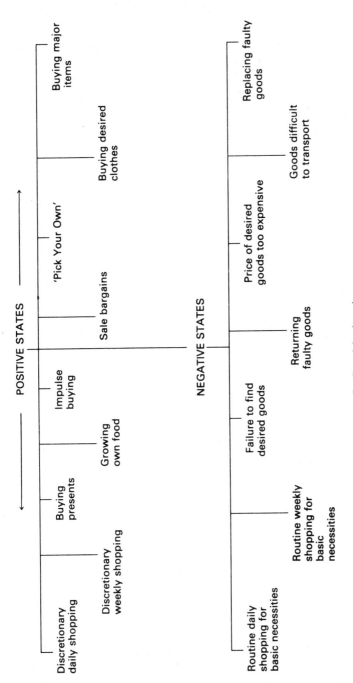

Figure 11.3 Provisioning time-states

- People are more comfortable working their way clockwise through a store, hence the main entrance to a supermarket should be located on the left-hand side of the building.
- Recognising the growing importance of the biological time-states, fruit, vegetables and other green products are located at the entrance to the store.
- Basic necessities which are essential, but boring products such as tea, sugar, milk are widely distributed so that the customer is 'led' past more exciting products. The latter have larger mark-ups than the former and also replace the negative time-state of the routine with the positive time-state of buying something one likes rather than needs.
- Aisle space varies with narrow aisles stocking familiar products which can be picked up at speed. Broader aisles are designed to slow customers down and encourage more leisurely browsing.
- Selected products are located to capture attention in one of the following ways:
    Eye-level shelves;
    End of aisle displays;
    Eye-level chiller cabinets;
    In longer rows than other products.

A major factor in customer psychology is the creation of brand loyalty. Supermarkets therefore pay increasing attention to promoting their own label goods by 'special offers'.

A 'value-added' through innovation or reducing any preparation time is an important competitive factor. Time once again becomes a competitive weapon, sometimes supplanting taste and price.

The 'themed merchandising concept' is the result of using *Gestalt* (sense of completeness) to attract the customer by placing in the same location a range of 'linked goods' such as 'All You Need for a Happy Easter'. This is another example of time-compression since customers will feel that 'everything they need' is to hand.

A major time challenge for supermarkets is accelerating the check-out process. Some possible ways are:

— All staff trained to check out;
— Goods move at time of selection direct to check-out chutes for pricing;
— Customers supplied with check-out calculators which 'read' all

bar codes as goods are selected. Any bar code not read will set off an alarm at the 'pay point'.

There is relatively little scope for any significant time-compression in supermarkets; the future lies with those who can provide more opportunities for time-layering. Possibilities are:

(a) Play centres for children while parents are at work, shopping, having a meal, or seeing a film.
(b) Home-management classes.
(c) Medical and paramedical services such as chiropodists on the premises.
(d) Hairdressing and beauticians on the premises.
(e) Grandparent caring.
(f) Car valeting while shopping.
(g) Minor car repairs while shopping.

In seeking for ideas on the improved packaging of provisioning time, supermarkets might look to department stores.

11.17 DEPARTMENT STORES

Department stores have been moving out of the provisioning time-zone into the leisure time-zone for some years; this trend will accelerate throughout the 1990s.

Department stores have changed from being emporia of shopping owned by one man whose name adorned the store, to being bazaars of specialist boutiques congregated under one roof. In this latter mode success depends on imposing a cohesion on the disparate parts so that customers feel they are dealing with a long-established 'store' rather than a series of shops.

Whereas people use supermarkets for time-compressing, they use department stores for making more long-term purchases. Sales assistants in supermarkets are expected to be conversant with the location of goods, in department stores a deeper level of product knowledge is expected. When judgements are asked for on the relative merits of goods, the department store assistant is expected to give an opinion in terms of relative quality rather than price.

Japanese department stores focus on three aspects of customer psychology which will be receiving increasing attention from their Western counterparts:

(1) Diversion
(2) Education
(3) Inducements

Diversion takes the form of providing for short-term leisure pursuits such as fishing. One Tokyo store has a stocked pool on the roof; customers can fish for about £5 for thirty minutes.

Much care is taken to educate customers in the use and care of purchases. Whereas in Western stores customers are bombarded with sales pitches on how to use the latest gadgets, little advice is offered after a purchase is made. By contrast, in Japanese stores you will have the services of a veterinary doctor if you decide to buy a pet. A kimono-clad sales assistant will give instruction on the proper wearing of kimonos. Stores follow the dictum that 'to sell goods it is also necessary to sell the knowledge required to use those goods'. This is an example of using service to reduce the risk of negative time often associated with trying out a product for the first time.

When it comes to inducements, younger customers in Japanese stores are encouraged to develop loyalty to a particular store. Children are given cards which are stamped at several check-points. A specified number of stamps wins a small prize. Teenagers are attracted to special teen departments by being offered 'club membership' privileges such as discounts and newsletters.

11.18　HOME SHOPPING

This should be the ultimate in time-layering, yet it has not proved as successful as its pioneers had hoped. Teleshopping took off in 1986 in the USA and boomed quickly.

Six major companies dominate the TV shopping scene in America:

(1) Home Shopping Network
(2) Cable Value Network
(3) QVC Network
(4) Shop Television Network
(5) J. C. Penney Shopping Network
(6) Sky Merchant

In Britain and Ireland, B Sky B is the major provider. Teleshopping has not taken hold in Europe. Each of the networks has a distinctive selling style, but all suffer from an image problem; they are perceived as purveyors of kitsch. Nevertheless, there are millions of US customers willing to order fake furs, powered tools and jewellery.

Home Shopping Network has an assertive selling style with fast-paced salesmen. QVC is more up-market and sells more national brands at a measured pace. Whereas Home Shopping Network gives viewers only a few minutes to order goods which have just been displayed on the screen, QVC has an easy plan and credit cards to make ordering less hectic. A recent innovation which has boosted sales is celebrity endorsements. Hollywood stars are shown wearing the jewellery on view.

This type of home shopping is relatively untested and is restricted largely to impulse buying. Longer established is buying from a mail-order catalogue. Long established in the United States by Sears Roebuck and in Britain by Littlewoods Stores, mail-order is once again growing in popularity as more women go out to work and have less time for shopping.

Both teleshopping and mail-order are examples of time-layering since purchase decisions can be made while relaxing at home, viewing television or having a bath. An example of time-compressing in the provisioning psychic time-zone is the growing use of store catalogues for previewing goods before making the purchasing decision. While many of the catalogues can be used for mail-order, they provide an opportunity to browse at home rather than in the store.

A final example of time-shaping is the growing practice of 'private views' for credit card holders. This enables regular customers to view goods in an evening when there are fewer crowds and more time to view. By the use of formal invitations, sherry receptions and musical performances, the trip to the store is shifted from the provisioning psychic time-zone to the leisure psychic time-zone.

11.19 POSITIVE AND NEGATIVE TIME STATES

People, especially women, spend more time (and money) in the provisioning psychic time-zone than in any other area of service.

Positive time-states in the provisioning psychic time-zone arise from satisfaction with purchases, particularly when they are discretionary or impulse buys. Even weekly shopping can be made attractive if there are diversions and opportunities for time-layering.

The great divide between the affluent West and Far East and the less affluent countries is in the availability and abundance of goods for sale in shops. Scarcity and restricted choice induce negative time-states in customers, the more so because they are usually accompanied by long, slow-moving queues. These provisioning problems of Eastern Europe, China and the underdeveloped world will take a long time to resolve. In the West the issues are much simpler. All that a supermarket or department store has to do to gain a competitive advantage is – as ever – to accentuate the positives and eliminate the negatives.

Accentuating the positives can be achieved through:

- Longer opening hours.
- More knowledgeable staff.
- Diversions to make shopping more exciting.
- Added-value through gift wrapping, discounts for store card holders and private views.
- Facilities to try on complete ensembles from head to toe without changing departments.
- Diversions for men while their partners are trying on clothes.
- More seating for elderly customers.

Eliminating the negatives can be achieved through:

— Adding excitement to essential shopping, e.g. a prize for purchasing a bag of sugar with a hidden number revealed at the check-out. (The prize might be that the customer does not pay for what is in their trolley.)
— Making an effort to track down the location of goods which are locally out of stock.
— Assistance with heavy loads or awkwardly shaped goods.
— No hassle replacement of faulty goods.
— Soliciting customers' ideas on improving service.

Supermarkets and department stores are not simply distribution centres of entertainment, enlightenment and care. In the caring 1990s, they will be judged not only on the quality and price of their goods but on other factors such as:

(a) How they help customers make the right choice to meet their needs.

(b) How they care for the young and the old accompanying their customers.
(c) How they forewarn regular customers of lack of stock so as not to waste their time.
(d) How they make shopping for anything an enjoyable experience.

Should they fail to meet these challenges, they may find that in ten years or so a growing number of customers will prefer to remain in the comfort and security of their homes and teleshop, thereby shaping their own time.

11.20 COMMUNICATIONS TIME ZONE

The development of man has been determined by his capacity to communicate. That capacity took a quantum leap forward in 1878 when the telephone came into practical use. This instrument heralded the dawn of the information technology revolution. The power of electricity became recognised about the same time, giving birth to transatlantic telegraphs, high-speed printing and eventually motion pictures, radio, television, the computer and the cellular phone.

All these are a long way from the tom-tom, smoke signals and hill telegraphs of previous eras. In terms of customer-time-care the communications psychic time-zone provides greater opportunities than any other for time-compressing and, to a lesser extent, time-shaping.

The distinguishing feature of this time-zone is that it enables man to acquire a god-like attribute – the ability to be in more than one place at the same time. It is this duality of time, this sense of bilocation, which influences customers' perceptions of communications products and services. Figure 11.4 provides examples of different communications time-states.

11.21 MOBILE COMMUNICATIONS

The cellular phone is the time-transforming product of the 1980s; it promises to be the revolutionary time-product of the 1990s. These instruments place the world at the fingertips of customers. There are currently four types of cellular phones:

(1) The mobile phone which is the original hard-wire phone fixed to a car. They usually offer hands-off operation and some operate by voice recognition.

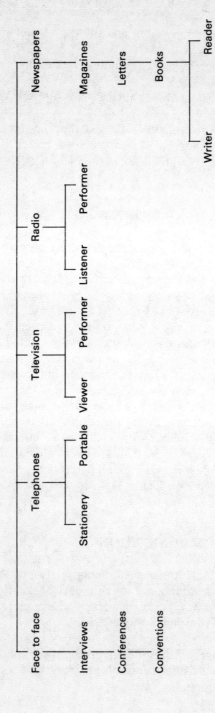

Figure 11.4 Communications time-states

(2) The transportable phone can be moved from car to car, but is too bulky to carry around.

(3) The bag phone is packed in a shoulder case; though easier to handle than the transportable, it is limited in its reach.

(4) The hand-held phone is the most popular; it can be carried in a coat pocket or attaché case. Its current limited range is being extended by advances in cellular electronics.

Personal communications networks (PCNs) are seen as a major advance in reducing the time necessary to contact another person. Hitherto, telephones have been fixed objects. When we telephone we establish contact with another location, not necessarily the person we want. PCNs will provide pocket-sized phones which people carry around, thus enabling the first truly person to person calls.

It has been estimated that in Britain half of all telephone calls fail to contact the desired person first time. Even a small improvement in first time contact would save significant amounts of time and money.

In Finland, the telephone service allows customers to use the same telephone number for all types of phones they use, be it fixed telephone, cellular phone or message pager. Calls are then redirected from one phone to another until contact is made. On the horizon is an 'intelligent' personal numbering system based on the concept of every person being given a personal phone number at birth. This would be encoded on a card which could be inserted into any telephone. Customers would be able to slot it into their home phone when at home, a mobile phone en route to somewhere, their work-place phone or their personal phone. To adapt an old advertising slogan – 'You're never alone with a phone'.

Such ease of communication will enable ambulances and other medical and emergency services to be summoned more quickly and given clearer directions to the location where they are needed, thus enabling more people to survive from illness or accidents. The intelligent personal numbering system is unlikely to come into operation until the mid-1990s, but there are other innovations which are much nearer:

— Telephone advisory services.
— Telephones for the deaf and blind.
— Selling by phone.

Telephone advisory services are of two types:

— Recorded
— Interactive

The growth of telephone advisory services was explosive in the 1980s. From religious inspiration to sexual stimulation, help is only a handset away. Recorded services provided general advice and comment; the attraction of such services is that they safeguard the anonimity of the caller, who can remain in the private psychic time-zone. Their disadvantage is what might be called the 'horoscope effect'; information seems in part relevant, but in reality is too generalised to be of real value.

Interactive calls range from 'chat-lines' linking a number of strangers, to sexual titillation and more edifying advice. The best example of such a service is the Samaritans, specially trained tele-counsellors. The use of the telephone by patients seeking therapy from their psychologist is a growing trend in the USA. There are mixed views on its efficacy, but it is likely to increase for one simple reason: people who can afford a course of psychoanalysis are usually busy. Their time is precious, therefore, if they feel they can benefit from therapy without making regular visits to the therapist, they will prefer to use the phone as their couch.

Helping the deaf use the telephone has gained increasing attention in recent years. Two types of approach are used – the text telephone and a relay telephone system. The text telephone is like a typewriter. Calls are made by connecting it to the telephone and typing a message. The relay system uses an operator to pass on information, using a monitor, a keyboard, a modem and special connection to the telephone. It works by the deaf person typing a message to the operator, who then rings the appropriate person and passes on the message. The reply is then conveyed to the deaf originator of the call by use of the text. Fax machines are likely to be more widely used by deaf people as the equipment comes down in price.

While, unlike deaf people, the blind can use ordinary telephones, the breakthrough for them will be facilities for telephone shopping and banking. Using tone-pads they will, in common with all other customers, be able to order groceries, swop money between accounts, pay bills without exposing themselves to the hazards of the increasingly crowded roads.

Telephone selling is another growth industry, and though it may have attractions for the housebound, the cost of the service means that it is usually highly priced goods which are being sold. The major disadvantage of telephone selling is that it intrudes into psychic time-zones when the customer is unlikely to be in the mood to buy anything. An unsolicited phone call which does not bring good news is always an intrusion; this creates a resistance barrier which is difficult for the seller to overcome. It is likely that telephone selling will be more successful in sales to companies. The receiver of the call is in the work psychic time-zone and is therefore likely to be more receptive to 'cold calls' selling work-related products and services.

11.22 INSTANT DATA

The phenomenal growth in the capabilities of computers makes feasible a new form of computerised literature which will transform our traditional use of libraries and books. The word 'computer' is misleading since it conveys a role based purely on numeracy rather than literacy. Computers can process words, pictures and sounds as well as numbers.

An article in *The Listener* (18 October 1990) by Benjamin Woolley provided an insight into the work of Ted Nelson an information sciences guru and deviser of the Xanadu project. This project has two components:

— Autodesk
— New Publishing Venture

Autodesk aims at providing a 'hypermedia server program' which will provide access to large computerised databases of information. Although mainly comprising texts there will also be video, music and voice databases. Individuals will be able to create new documents by creating links between the content of existing ones. People will be able to create their own databases, enabling them to gain access to the information they need more swiftly.

The New Publishing Venture will consist of networks of the databases, widening individual access and giving more opportunities for time-compressing. References made in an academic text, for instance, could enable the network to take the reader direct to the source of the reference which in turn could lead to the sources of other references; all in a matter of minutes.

A whole new service industry would come into being offering personalised databases. The suppliers could be franchised in common with the trend in other service industries.

Worldwide news coverage is another form of instant access to data. The use of communications satellites enables individuals to be completely up to date in what is happening across the globe.

An intriguing example of the power of satellites to reconstruct time was the decision in 1990 of the Tuareg – the largest tribe of nomads in the Sahara Desert – to delay their annual migration for the first time in their history. The reason for the ten day delay was their wish to view the final episode of the American soap opera, *Dallas*.

11.23   SIMULATING REALITY

Possibly the most intriguing development associated with computer science is advances in simulation. Pilots can 'experience' turning off the wrong engine, surgeons can 'experience' the effects of removing the wrong organ without suffering the consequences of their mistakes. Simulators permit time-warps to be experienced vicariously.

In airlines, simulators have long been used for training air crew and are being developed in the training of heart surgeons, undersea oil explorers and others who dice with death in their day-to-day activities in the work psychic time-zone. Hitherto, one drawback of simulators has been that they cannot completely simulate reality. The brain passes on the message that 'this is not really happening'.

Now, using computers and sophisticated communications devices, it is possible to create 'virtual reality'. The main components for transferring individuals into a state of virtual reality are a helmet and a glove. The helmet, which costs millions of dollars, comprises two tiny liquid crystal screens which cover each eye and completely envelop the user's field of vision with stereoscopic three-dimensional images. Sensors monitor the movement of the head and as the head moves the images change. Headphones convey sounds appropriate to the images. To all intents the individual is in a new world – a computer-generated reality.

The 'datagloves' are electronic gloves wired to be sensitive to movements of the wearer's fingers. By flexing the fingers the wearer can 'move' in the image being projected by the screens. This could be the cockpit of a spacecraft, a room, an office, or a museum. The 'movements' could involve running, jumping, or even flying around a room.

Virtual reality interacts with the brain and nervous system which fill in any gaps in 'reality'. The normal limits of the body disappear. The wearer can become huge or minute – master or mistress of the universe.

Still at an early stage of development for civilian use, the possibilities of virtual reality for time-shaping are incalculable. In theory it will be possible to visit the world's museums, attend a business conference across the globe, experience life on Mars; all without moving from your armchair.

11.24 AUTOMATING CUSTOMER-TIME-CARE

Much nearer in terms of improved customer-time-care are advances in communications science affecting two worldwide industries – airlines and financial services. Both these industries invested heavily in communications technology in the 1970s and 1980s. Both have ambitious plans for the 1990s.

In the airlines there is a variety of innovations which will lead to time-compressing:

- Automatic ticket machines to enable passengers to buy a ticket and receive a boarding card in less than a minute.
- Touch-screen multilanguage information facilities.
- Use of hand-held minicomputers to check passengers in on the spot, without the tedium of waiting in line.
- Direct booking of seats from home with automated debit to the bank and check-in by thumb print.
- Introduction of an automatic ticket and boarding pass (ATB) which does away with the multicoupon ticket.
- Aircraft communications addressing and reporting system (ACARS) which will improve communications in flight between air crew and ground staff, resulting in quicker turn arounds and shorter check-in times.
- Integrated cabin management system (ICMS) which, by using a central computer on the aircraft linked to the ground via satellite, enables passengers using 'personal' video screens on the backs of seats facing them to arrange hotels, have flowers sent to loved ones, purchase goods by mail-order. Payment will be made automatically by a credit card 'swipe reader' built into the system. This is 'time-layering' with a vengeance.

Less glamorous, though no less dramatic, are communications developments in the financial services industry:

- Customer activated terminals (CATs) will overtake automated teller machines, providing a wide range of services, using touch and coloured screens as well as multilanguage production facilities.
- Home banking via tone-pad and voice response round the clock.
- International networks of ATMs which can be accessed by one card of any of the participating banks.
- More opportunities for electronic payments at points of sales (EFTPOS) such as all night garages.
- 'Smart cards' with embedded microchips which can enable a wide variety of banking transactions to be performed and also hold personal data (such as blood group).

11.25 CONCLUSION

In the 1990s, humankind will spend more time in the 'communications psychic time-zone' than in previous decades. More than any other, this zone provides opportunity for time-compressing, time-layering, time-plexing. The speed of technological change is getting faster than the ability of man to assimilate it. There is a danger that what is a tool can become a master. Computer literacy will become one of the most important competencies. In many societies, divisions traditionally based on class, religion and race will be replaced by a schism between the computer literates and illiterates.

Manufacturers of computer-related products and providers of computer-based services will need to include provision for customer education, and price advantages for the computer literate on whom they have to spend less time. Unlike the poor, computer illiterates need not always be with us.

12 Two Passage of Time-zones – the Chronological and the Durable

12.1 INTRODUCTION

Man seeks identity by relating his place in history to what has passed and to what is likely in the future. This accounts for his interest in the chronological psychic time-zone. Man also seeks to gain maximum benefit from the time investment he has had to make in order to acquire things. This accounts for his interest in the durability psychic time-zone.

Providers of goods and services in both zones are therefore concerned with satisfying the needs of customers which relate to the past or the future, rather than the here and now.

12.2 THE CHRONOLOGICAL TIME-ZONE

Awareness of this psychic time-zone is exemplified in such descriptions as:

— Old fashioned
— Historic
— Traditional
— Behind the times
— Before its time
— Ahead of its time
— Futuristic
— New Age

Figure 12.1 gives examples of choronological time-states. Within the psychic time-zone there are two types of time:

- Retro-time involves going back to a previous time in history.
- Forward time involves projections into the future.

214

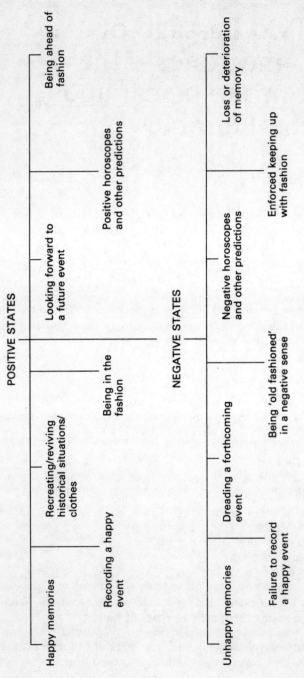

Figure 12.1 Chronological time-states

There are many products and services which use chronological time perspectives to attract and sell to the customer. Typical advertisements were quoted in Table 6.1. It is only in the twentieth century that humankind has been able to experience voices and moving images from the past. The phonograph, movie camera and now the camrecorder are instruments which enable customers to enjoy retro-time.

Computer sciences provide opportunities for historical simulations, whereby the purchaser of a 'war game' software package can pretend to be one of the major players of the Second World War – Adolf Hitler, Josef Stalin, Harry Truman or Winston Churchill, take your choice.

More realistic representations are played out in real life as people dress and behave in the manner of their ancestors for the amusement of tourists. From the Polynesian Cultural Centre in Hawaii to the Viking Centre in Dublin, people can experience the past. Those preferring the future can visit the NASA Space Centre in Houston, Texas, the park of Technological and Economic Department in Moscow, or Disney World in Tokyo.

Theme parks are a major chronological time industry of the twentieth century. Other chronological products and services are:

(a) Photography – caters for retro-time and preserves happy memories; everyone takes photographs at weddings, no one takes them at funerals. Why?
(b) Classical drama – reproduces the entertainment of previous times. 'Modern dress' versions of the classics are rarely popular since they create a time distortion in the mind of the audience.
(c) Museums and art galleries are custodians of the artefacts of the past and enable customers to indulge in retro-time.

The biggest single industry catering for the chronological psychic time-zone is clothing. Apart from the ritual psychic time-zone and to some extent the work psychic time-zone, people wear clothes to make a statement. In Nigeria the statement may relate to tribal allegiances, in India to caste, in many countries to religious affiliation. All such statements have a 'traditional' dimension to them, be it the turban of sikhs or the bonnets of Amish women. But in most of Western society the statement relates to 'fashion', the prevailing custom in dress.

Customers (particularly women) fall into four categories:

(1) Trend-setters
(2) Conformists
(3) Disintereteds
(4) Transcendants

Trend-setters are those who can tolerate a gap between present time and forward time. They adopt a mode copied by a significant number of others.

Conformists are those who can tolerate only a small gap between present time and forward time. They form the largest segment of the fashion markets. They need reassurance that the step into forward time will not expose them to ridicule.

Disinteresteds are those for whom clothes protect the body, rather than project an image. They buy 'out of fashion' or secondhand clothes with no intention of making a fashion statement. Ironically, their 'statement' may be the loudest of all, though it does little to help the 'rag trade'.

Transcendants are those whose point of reference is beyond current fashion. It may be that they are more oriented to retro-time than forward time. Not for them the latest craze; they prefer 'classic' clothes which suggest individuality and a link with a prosperous past. 'Soignée, but not sophisticated' is what they would like chiselled on their tombstone.

Fashion, of course, extends beyond clothes; it embraces furniture, jewellery, housing, cars and much else. The markets for antiques, old masters and impressionists are fuelled by the desire to enjoy retro-time. Concorde, streamlined cars and space travel are equally fuelled by the desire for forward time. The opportunities and hazards of operating in the chronological psychic time-zone are illustrated by the author's experience of a combined Orient Express–Concorde trip to Venice in October 1986.

12.3   DESIGNING A TIME PACKAGE

The Orient Express trip from London to Venice, returning by Concorde, is one of the best examples of products and services being blended to provide a unique time package. An analysis of the components in terms of psychic time-zones and time-states illustrates its strengths and its pitfalls.

In the early 1980s the carriages of the Orient Express of the

Wagon-Lits company were restored to their former glory. Designed for the journey between Paris and Istanbul between the two world wars, the carriages were left to rot after the Second World War. Interest in the Orient Express was rekindled in the 1960s by the success of the film adaptation of Agatha Christie's thriller *Murder on the Orient Express*. This reminded a worldwide audience of times when rail travel was slower and more elegant. Passengers dressed for dinner, ate exotically and passed the time in a sumptuously decorated bar, listening to a pianist in black tie and white dinner jacket. The film influenced perceptions of viewers and, in a sense, froze the Orient Express and its passengers in a time capsule.

Cashing in on the interest created by the film, a consortium put together a package as follows:

- Leave London by Pullman at 10 a.m. on day one.
- Transfer from Pullman at Folkestone to a ferry with its separate 'Orient Express' lounge.
- Board the Orient Express in Boulogne and retire to private compartments for two.
- Travel by train to Venice arriving in the evening of day two.
- Transported to an elegant, long-established hotel in Venice.
- Spend three days at the hotel.
- Fly from Venice to London by Concorde on day three.

(The option of completing the trip in reverse order was available.)

Despite, or perhaps because of, the high price, the trip has proved successful. It is easy to see why, once each part of the 'package' is analysed in terms of time.

First, the motivation of most people going on the trip is to celebrate an important event in family time:

— Honeymoon
— Significant wedding anniversary (usually 25th)
— Graduation

The train journey is satisfying the need for chronological time, rather than travel time. There are quicker ways of getting to Venice. The time-state involved at this stage is retro-time, going back to the past. This is reinforced by the choice of clothes passengers wear on the train. They tend to hark back to the 1920s. (Despite the fact that the original train operated over three decades, it is the clothes associated with the Agatha Christie film which predominate.)

In addition to providing chronological time and travel time, the train journey also provides leisure time. The dominant time-states in this psychic zone are:

(a) Relaxation
(b) Luxury eating
(c) Reading time
(d) Touring time as the train goes through the different countries en route to Venice.

Leisure time and chronological time are the dominant psychic time-zones during the stay in Venice. The hotels used by the travellers are both luxurious and evoke a sense of the past.

When the time comes to return to London the use of Concorde presents some interesting time factors:

- Although it is the fastest civil aircraft in the world, the journey from Venice to London takes up to an hour *longer* than the normal air journey. This is because Concorde has to follow a flight path along the Mediterranean and into the Bay of Biscay in order to fly faster than the speed of sound without causing noise pollution over inhabited areas. Therefore, the use of Concorde is not primarily to supply travel time.
- The dominant psychic time-zone is chronological time, the time-state being future time.
- Whereas the scheduled Atlantic flights of Concorde are predominantly in the travel psychic time-zone and work psychic time-zone, the Venice/London flight is predominantly satisfying leisure and chronological time.
- Ironically, the clock time during which the plane exceeds the speed of sound is less than a quarter of the journey.

To summarise, the Orient Express/Venice/Concorde trip layers the following psychic time-zones:

— Travel (both 'slow' and 'fast');
— Chronological (both past and future);
— Leisure (both relaxation and sightseeing);
— Family (both honeymooners and long-married);

— Life maintenance (both essential and luxury meals).
Unfortunately, there can be 'interruptions' which distract from
the positive aspects of time-states within each zone:

- The journey to Folkestone by Pullman is short and the meal is
  therefore served too early and can be rushed.
- The Transfer to the ferry at Folkestone is a discontinuity. Despite
  the special lounge, other passengers use common facilities and
  gawp at those whose clothes may be appropriate to early times, but
  are literally 'out of place' and time-state.
- The carriages are cramped with insufficient space for suitcases
  carrying formal wear as well as other clothes. This introduces a
  chore element into what is intended to be leisure time.
- The one bar on the train can only accommodate one-fifth of the
  passengers, with the result that leisure is interrupted by overcrowding and scrambling for seats.
- The sleeping bunks are uncomfortable; this is made worse by the
  carriages and the engine being of very different generations.
- Arriving at Venice, one leaves the opulence of time past, to be met
  by two groups each in a different psychic time-zone. The crew of
  the train from chef to carriage attendant are lined up to shake the
  hands of those passengers wishing to continue in retro-time. Behind the crew is a gaggle of couriers holding up hastily scrawled
  signs with the names of various hotels and treating the cosseted
  passengers as cattle. Suddenly the psychic time-zone is 'waiting'.
- The return journey by Concorde also suffers from indicators that
  passengers are not genuine Concorde users. The manner of the
  cabin crew is typical of a charter flight, indifferent and hurried. To
  reinforce this time displacement, the passengers have thrust at
  them on arrival at Heathrow a 'Concorde pack' which would have
  added value during the flight, but which, faced with the hassle of
  baggage retrieval, is simply a reminder that the 'good time' is over
  and that the 'Concorde experience' is viewed by the airline as an
  inconvenience, or rather that the passenger is.

The lesson of the Orient Express/Concorde package is that the
total experience must be designed if the customer is to feel wholly
satisfied. Special care has to be taken at points of discontinuity such
as moving from train to hotel, from hotel to aircraft. The layering of
psychic time-zones must be carefully considered in relation to
changes in time-states. Leisure becomes a chore when a bar is

overcrowded and when there are long waits for transport. Time-warps occur when there is an instant contrast in the demeanour of elegant train crew and scruffy, noisy couriers. The designer has to empathise with the customers and ensure that the Concorde experience is delivered in a way that reinforces the time-state of future time and not deteriorate into a charade in the here and now.

12.4   THE DURABILITY TIME-ZONE

Preservation of the desirable is the hallmark of the durability psychic time-zone. More than elsewhere, manufacturers and providers of services are judged on the fulfilment of their promise that something will last. In the 1990s, this psychic time-zone will preoccupy more and more customers who want recycled products and the minimal durability of undesired materials such as plastics. The old adage that customers buy the packaging rather than the product is likely to be turned on its head as environmentally aware customers reject excessive packaging.

Figure 12.2 illustrates some positive and negative durability time-states. Customers seek products and services which will keep them in the positive time-states. Unfortunately, sustaining the durability of a product generally involves life-maintaining chores:

— Cleaning shoes;
— Regular servicing and cleaning of motor cars;
— Painting walls;
— Dry cleaning clothes and curtains;
— Visiting the dentist.

These are but a few examples of the needs of customers which can be satisfied in this zone. The whole concept of 'guarantees' relate to the durability time-zone; breakdowns of equipment are examples of time distortions. Customers want to avoid these and are willing to pay a premium for extended guarantee periods or after sales service agreements. Building the costs of these into a product price can provide a perception of added-value which has a greater psychic impact than making separate charges.

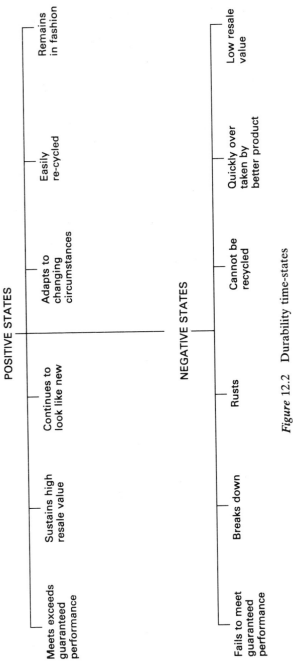

Figure 12.2   Durability time-states

12.5   NEW CONCEPTS OF DURABILITY

In the 1990s, customer-time-care in the durability zone will mean more than reliable performance. Once again, Japan is leading the way. Japanese car manufacturers recognise that product reliability in terms of engine performance and bodywork is taken for granted by their customers. Competition now has to be based on a new concept – *miryokuteki hinshitu* – making cars that fascinate, surprise, give pleasure. Maintaining the 'delight factor' over the performing life of the car is the new objective.

Design is directed at giving each model a distinctive personality or 'feel'. When defect-free cars are commonplace, quality issues revolve around those little extra touches that convey a concern for customer care. Improved visibility, smoother suspension and doors that close silently all help to make customers feel good, both physically and psychologically.

Recognising that the durability of the occupants must take precedence over the durability of the vehicle, new safety devices are receiving prime attention. Air bags for drivers and passengers and seat belts using pressurised gas to grasp tight in a crash are two examples of 'exclusive extras' which will become normal features of cars.

Psychology plays as big a role as engineering in the design of these more durable vehicles. Fifteen product-development engineers in Honda spent a year identifying an image to personify a new family sedan. They eventually came up with a rugby player in a suit; in other words, a strong athletic gentleman.

The next step was to articulate some traits which the car should display. One of these was 'stress free'. This resulted in new ways of reducing noise and vibration. Greater attention is also being given to the durability of internal car furnishings and equipment. The intention is that the car should look and feel like new throughout its performing life.

12.6   CONCLUSION

Both the chronological and durable psychic time-zones are in their relative infancy. Both will receive a boost in their importance to customers in the 1990s.

Customers will want to spend more time in the chronological zone as we get closer to one of the rarest of chronological milestones – the new millennium. Interest in keeping links with the past and attempting to foresee the future will boost visits to historic sites and purchases of futuristic products. A characteristic of the advent of a millennium is that it stimulates thinking in terms of a thousand years rather than the more common units of decades and centuries.

This long-term perspective will influence customer care psychology in the durability zone, where concern about the durability of the planet and of the human race will influence patterns of behaviour and consumer choice. Those manufacturers and service providers who are sensitive to these emerging concerns and can transform them into positive time-states will endure. Those who pay lip-service or only scant attention to the new values, needs and expectations of customers will suffer a durability problem.

13 The Biological Time-zone

13.1 INTRODUCTION

All of us live in this psychic time-zone; it governs our health and longevity.

Over the past century there have been staggering increases in life expectancy across the developed countries. There is a growing body of medical opinion which says that this trend will continue and result in people living as long as trees. Studies on life expectancy have tended to focus on past trends in mortality. These prognoses of a continuing increase in longevity have been challenged by the findings of researchers at the University of Chicago and Argonne National Laboratory, Illinois. Writing in *Science* magazine (November 1990) the researchers make the following predictions:

- The gradual rundown of the body will counteract any significant increases in the life-span of people over 85.
- Alzheimer's disease which accelerates the onset of senility and degenerative diseases such as deafness, blindness and arthritis, will become more prevalent as more people survive beyond 85.
- To increase American life expectancy to 100 would require reductions in the mortality rate of over 85 per cent.
- Everyone is affected by some fundamental rate of ageing of the organs, muscles, bones and flesh.

These predictions of a levelling off of mortality rates have great significance for those who provide products and services in the biological time-zone. As we saw in Chapter 3, the growth of the 'old old' customer is a significant factor for all concerned with manufacturing goods and providing services.

13.2 POSITIVE BIOLOGICAL TIME-STATES

There are five clusters of positive time-states and at least nine negative time-states which affect customers (see Figure 13.1). The positive clusters are:

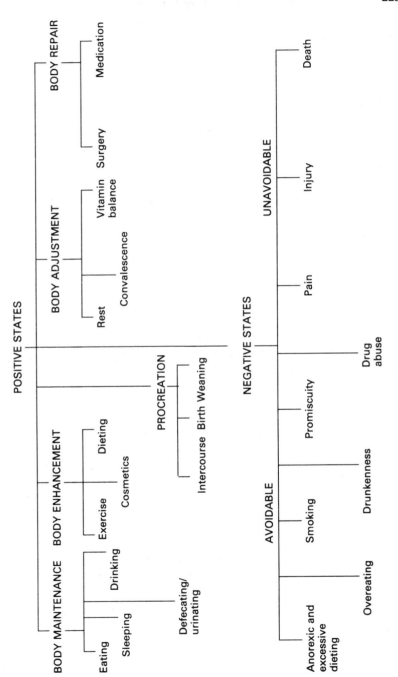

Figure 13.1 Biological time-states

(1) Body maintenance
(2) Body enhancement
(3) Procreation
(4) Body adjustment
(5) Body repair

In the body maintenance time-states people perform activities demanded by the brain and other organs:
(a) Eating
(b) Drinking
(c) Sleeping
(d) Defecating
(e) Urinating

Frequency of responding to these basic needs varies with age and between individuals, but many people view these activities as a waste of time and seek to 'layer' them whenever possible. Reading the paper at breakfast; travelling overnight in a sleeping berth; having a supply of reading materials and a radio in the bathroom are all examples of this desire to 'layer' time.

In more recent years, 'breakfast television' has become part of the layering process; though there are few toilets in which one will find a television, perhaps because it can be perceived as a prying eye on very personal functions.

In body maintenance time-states, customer care psychology has to be directed at satisfying the desire for speed of accomplishment and also for 'hygiene' both physical and psychic. Japan has given a lead here by developing an automatic flushing and sterilising loo with a heated seat. Also on its way is a 'paperless' loo which integrates a bidet into the toilet; when necessary, a robotic arm shoots up a stream of warm water followed by a gust of hot air directed at the appropriate area.

'Psychic' hygiene is also taken care of by the Japanese; the loos play music to mask any untoward sounds. If the undesirable sounds are too loud they can be drowned out by a small portable machine which makes flushing noises.

Customers, while in the biological psychic time-zone, are more health conscious than ever before. This means that all involved in the harvesting, processing and cooking of food have to be seen to be more conscious than ever of their own hygiene. Supermarkets, restaurants and food factories will need to provide staff with spotless uniforms, gloves while handling food, touch free taps and toilet flushing.

'Healthy' foods will loom larger on customer shopping lists as we have seen in Chapter 11 on the Provisioning Psychic Time Zone.

The body enhancement time-state is devoted to keeping at bay the ageing process. For customers in this time-state their need is reassurance that in both face and body they are conquering the ravages of biological time. In the past, manufacturers of body enhancement products such as diet foods, and providers of body enhancement services such as exercise machines have tended to make exaggerated claims, resulting in dissatisfaction. Promises such as 'You'll look lovelier than ever'; 'You'll lose so much weight even your friends won't recognise you' will create expectations which cannot be met.

Customer care psychology will in future focus on self-image in this time-state, with greater emphasis on how the customer will feel within themselves rather than how they will appear to others. Once again, time-layering will come into play to counteract the boredom of exercise. Many appliances will have built in radios or cassette players so that an individual can keep up to date on news or enjoy music while exercising.

Cosmetic surgery will increase at both ends of the age spectrum. Children will be given changes to their features to make them more in line with the idealised image of their parents; the elderly will pay to look younger. Associated with this trend will be a growth in cosmetics for niche markets such as children, the old old and ethnic groups.

To save time in choosing perfumes for each occasion and to lengthen the durability of perfume throughout an evening, clothes will be impregnated with 'appropriate' perfumes.

The procreation time-state is, in a sense, the most important for customer care psychology since without it there would be no customers. Procreation brings in its wake a great variety of goods and services; from nappies to nannies, from babyfoods to toys. The key factor to bear in mind in customer care psychology is that for parents (particularly with the first child) they are undergoing a common but unique experience. Common for the provider of goods and services, unique for the parents.

There are two areas of opportunity for those involved in supplying or serving those in the procreation time-state:

- Special services for the one-parent family, who, if employed, is under considerable time pressures and therefore seeks opportunities for time-compressing and time-layering.
- Development of the 'great grandparents' market with cards and gifts which mark them off as a distinctive niche.

The body adjustment time-state is the time people need to adjust to new circumstances. After hard physical exercise there is a need for rest; after a major operation there is a need for convalescence; moving to a different country may require supplementing the local diet with vitamins and salt tablets. In an increasingly hectic world people need to spend a higher proportion of their time in the body adjustment time-state, this means that 'rest rooms' will have to live up to their name, rather than be a euphemism for toilets. Shops, banks, stations and airports will be required to provide more seating as customers live longer.

Greater attention will be given to the design of chairs, beds and other resting appliances, in terms of their biological impact. A selling point will be the 'comfort time-span'; resulting in the 'six hour' chair, the 'ten hour' bed.

The body repair time-state is that in which an individual seeks to have corrected some damage to or failure of a critical organ, bone or tissue. In this psychic time-zone, the individual undergoes a transformation for the better. As individuals give greater attention to body maintenance, body enhancement and body adjustment there will be less need to spend time in the body repair state.

13.3 NEGATIVE BIOLOGICAL TIME-STATES

Broadly speaking, these can be classified as 'avoidable' and 'unavoidable'; what they have in common is that they damage the mind/body and therefore accelerate ageing and shorten longevity. Avoidable time-states are:

- Anorexia and excessive dieting – these have their roots in the psyche; they are the consequence of distorting the body enhancement time-state. They can be looked on as the result of unrealistic time-compression; brain time and body time out of sync.
- Overeating often has its roots in the psyche; an attempt to compensate for some perceived failure. It can be considered a failure in

time-layering; overindulgent business lunches; eating because the food is there; consuming food at a party as a substitute for failure to make social contact.

- Smoking is often an addiction, but it can also be a confidence prop or a timing mechanism. Smoking is always associated with time-layering; the act of smoking does not take place in isolation from some other activity. Addicted smokers have a health problem; confidence prop smokers and 'pacing smokers' have less of a health problem, but like the addicted are a hazard to others. 'Pacing smokers' are those who use the smoking of a cigarette as a means of passing time rather than a source of nicotine satisfaction.

- Drunkenness and drug abuse, like smoking, harms both the affected person and others. In terms of customer care psychology, they can be viewed as a means of modifying negative time into positive time which in the end fail since time is obliterated from the psyche. Because society views drunkenness and drug abuse as time-wasters and in many cases 'time-intruders' into others' time enjoyment, the providers of alcohol and non-ethical drugs will come under increasing pressure to:

— reduce or stop production;
— provide non-harmful substitutes;
— bear the cost of the adverse effects of their products and services.

- Promiscuity is not listed here on moral grounds, but because it represents a negative time-state which can adversely affect the longevity of those involved. Aids is one consequence of promiscuous activity, abortion, abandoned children and to some degree child abuse are other consequences. In the language of customer psychology, promiscuity is a begetter of time-warps. A healthy, natural act of love and care performed in a positive mind-state suddenly changes into a negative time-state, damaging the mind and bodies of those involved and of innocents.

- Injury, pain and death are negative time-states whether or not they are self-inflicted. Their existence changes the time-state not only of the sufferer but of others, usually for the worse. Medical services and pharmaceutical companies are at the forefront of reducing the adverse effects of injury and pain and of staving off the ultimate time-killer – death. In terms of customer care psychology none of these states will be completely eliminated; all that suppliers of goods and services can do is attempt to reduce their negative impact.

13.4   THE BUSINESS IMPLICATIONS OF THE BIOLOGICAL TIME-ZONE

There are four major trends in the biological psychic time-zone which need to be taken into account in applying customer care psychology:

(1) The growing awareness of the symbiosis of man and nature.
(2) The desire for quick feedback of biological data.
(3) The increasing numbers of disabled customers.
(4) The power of the old old customer.

Care of the environment has moved from a concern in the 1980s to an obsession in the 1990s. People are more aware of the interdependence of the human being and nature. This symbiosis of the survival of each depending on the other is illustrated in the increasing attention which service industries are giving to environmental issues, as was shown in Chapter 2. Manufacturing industries are even more affected by the ecological symbiosis. Restrictions on environmentally unfriendly manufacturing processes are increasing; the demand for environmentally friendly goods is growing swiftly. All this will increase prices at least in the medium term as old processes, amortised over many years, are replaced by new ones calling for high levels of investment. Customer psychology will need to be directed at convincing customers of a genuine concern for their health and that of the environment. Gimmicks and a profusion of 'green' labelling will simply lose customers who in this instance are as much concerned about 'cosmic time' as with more immediate time zones.

While glancing at the cosmos, people are even more preoccupied with glancing at their watches. We live in a 'now' era where people want time-compression in access to data. This is particularly true of their personal biological data. As a consequence, there is a growing demand for products and services which tell the customer the 'good' or 'bad' news as soon as possible. Associated with this is a move to home-based self-service, replacing the requirement to seek professional advice at a particular time and place convenient to the service provider rather than the customer.

Self-administered pregnancy tests have long been on the market. They are an example of time-compression with consequences for other psychic time-zones such as private time and waiting time. Examples of instant feedback products are:

(a) Portable computers which calculate alcohol intake thus reducing the chances of drink/drive accidents.
(b) Portable blood pressure monitors which at the touch of a finger give readings of both pulse rate and blood pressure.
(c) Pedometers which automatically calculate the distance a walker, jogger or runner covers and gives a read-out on speed and stamina.
(d) Electric scales which keep track of body fat as well as weight.

When it comes to personal services for customers in the biological psychic time-zone the choice can be bewildering. Each of the following are examples of devices for time-compressing. They reduce the time which customers would otherwise have to spend in both the travel and waiting psychic time-zones. They also provide more opportunities for time-layering than would otherwise exist. For example, it could be possible to learn a language on tape while performing most of the following services at home; this would not be feasible at other locations:

- Needle free electrolysis enables hair to be removed from areas where it is not wanted.
- Exercise machines which integrate a variety of equipment to provide a 'gym' in a small space.
- First aid kit for teeth which enables an individual to make emergency repairs including replacing a filling.
- Home massager which replicates the touch of a trained masseur.
- Electrical manicure set which also acts as a pedicure.
- Transcutaneous electrical nerve stimulator which claims to increase blood flow and increase the level of endorphines – the body's natural defence against pain.
- Stress gum which, when chewed, reacts with the $_pH$ level of the body to indicate, when the gum is inspected, whether there is stress (green) or no stress (pink).

As home-based personal biological services become more prevalent, professional services in the biological psychic time-zone will become more specialised and more expensive. There will also be the growth of more support groups to help individuals move from the negative time-states to the positive. Another development will be the growth of personal coaches and paramedics. Coaches will act as the conscience of the individual in the time-states of body enhancement and body adjustment. Paramedics will operate in the latter time-state and also in body repair. Although they will have spent fewer years on medical studies than the traditional family doctor, paramedics will be at least as knowledgeable on common ailments and will have ready access to specialist opinion via telecommunications links with medical data banks and consultants. The traditional family doctor will disappear, moving on to be a consultant or moving back into the ranks of the paramedics.

Progress in the biological psychic time-zone will enhance the life expectancy of those born with some disability. The disabled (or the 'challenged' as they are likely to be called) will form a powerful customer pressure group. All providers of services, particularly those operating in the travel and leisure psychic time-zones, will be expected to respond to the needs and expectations of the disabled in terms of access, specially designed facilities, and integration into theatres, cinemas and other leisure centres. Customer care psychology will need to address such issues as:

— Dealing in a 'normal manner' with the disabled.
— Providing special care in an unobtrusive way.
— Designing goods which will make it easier for disabled people to perform routine tasks.
— Employing an increasing number of disabled in customer contact roles.

Among the products and services developed for the 'disabled market' will be:

• Voice activated typewriters which respond to voice patterns and the text can be edited and printed using only the individual's voice. This will be of great assistance to those with limb or muscular problems.
• Voice keys which operate in response to a spoken personal identification number and password which is in line with a recorded voice pattern. This will be of real benefit to blind and/or arthritic people.
• Devices to improve hearing, such as surgically implanted speech processors which convert sound into digital form which is then decoded and transmitted to the inner ear.

All the above products expand the time capabilities of the disabled, either by speeding up an activity such as typewriting, reducing wasted time spent fumbling for a key hole, or enabling time-layering by allowing the deaf to 'hear' while performing other tasks.

Many of the products for the disabled will also benefit the old old. The increasing power of this group was discussed in Chapter 3. Apart from issues of care, the purchasing power of the old old guarantees that their needs will receive increasing attention. Among the trends will be:

(a) Products which are easy to unpackage.
(b) Directions written in large type.
(c) Hearing reinforcers in cinemas and theatres.
(d) Smaller portions of meals in restaurants.
(e) Personal alarm systems.
(f) Safe 'hot water' bottles which are sealed and filled with a re-usable non-toxic gel which takes only a few minutes to heat up in a microwave oven and stays hot for hours. (Alternatively, it can be used as a medical 'cold pack' after freezing.)
(g) Alertness stimulators which can be battery operated and release measured doses of certain oils, such as juniper, basil, peppermint and rosemary into the atmosphere, helping to reduce stress and anxiety in a car or elsewhere.

13.5 CONCLUSION

The biological psychic time-zone is central to Customer care psychology since it determines the health, both physical and mental, of the customer. While existing in the biological psychic time-zone the customer is making choices on matters of body maintenance, body enhancement, body adjustment and body repair, as well as, from time to time, procreation.

Counteracting these choices are others which can lead to a shortening of one's biological time-span. Many products and services are aimed at helping people make these choices.

The desire to remain in the biological psychic time-zone as long as possible has given rise to a relatively new service industry – cryonics. This service seeks to transport people who have died to a time when a cure for their fatal illness is available.

The process involves taking a body down to the temperature of liquid nitrogen so that the brain structure is preserved. The body remains stored until the time (possible several centuries hence) when a cure has been found for the particular ailment. Then the body is unfrozen and after appropriate medical attention is returned to life. The cost of having the body frozen is around £600 000; if a person decides to have only the head frozen, the cost drops to £21 000.

Still in its infancy, cryonics has nevertheless attracted some actual and potential customers. This could be used to support the argument that the only service people seek is time and more time. Fortunately, there is more verifiable proof to be found in the analysis of other psychic time-zones.

14 The Benefits of the Customer-time-care Approach

14.1 INTRODUCTION

It has long been the cry of those involved in the 'service quality revolution' that companies which embark on the road to higher standards of customer care have begun a never-ending journey. Unfortunately, more and more companies have come to a jarring halt or have slowed down to a crawl in their endeavours to establish and sustain ever increasing standards. Metaphorically footsore and bleeding, they ask 'Where next?'; 'What more can we do?' There are always pathfinders around to suggest an easier or quicker route. 'Buy this package'; 'Adapt this technique and all will be well.' Oh that it were so simple!

Devising ever higher standards of customer care is not an achieving process, but a striving process; the achievement comes from continuing to strive. One of the main benefits of the customer-time-care approach is that it provides a box of tools to sustain the striving.

14.2 CARING FOR TIME/TIME FOR CARING

Time is life/life is time. Time is money/money is time. These juxtapositions highlight another benefit of the approach. Time is important to everyone regardless of gender, race or creed. Therefore, the approach has a global application in expressing care.

Even the poorest can give their time to the service of another. Caring is not simply an act of giving donations; it is an act of giving time and attention to the needs of another. The distinction between serving and caring is subtle, but vital: 'service' is the performance of a contractual obligation (however loosely defined); 'care' is a manifestation of concern to satisfy the needs of another.

At the heart of the customer-time-care approach is concern with helping others make the best possible use of their time. From this central thesis there flow many channels of time which individuals may

235

need to be helped to navigate if they are to have a fulfilling voyage through life.

Customer care psychology is concerned with the study of what motivates people to experience different levels of satisfaction from their choice of goods and services. In Part I we considered what might be called 'the conventional wisdom'. Factors like value for money, reliability, courtesy and many others undoubtedly have a part to play. They are the conscious factors in the psychology of customer care. With Part II we move into the subconscious and see that there is one common link which binds virtually all goods and services together; their perceived contribution to influencing a customer's most precious possession – time.

14.3   A NEW PARADIGM

Customer-time-care is not a new 'package'; it is a new paradigm – a different way of ensuring maximum satisfaction for customers. It opens up new vistas of opportunity to both manufacturers and providers of services. It prompts answers to such questions as:

— What psychic time-zones do we operate in?
— What opportunities are there for penetrating other psychic time-zones?
— What psychic time-zones do our customers want to be in?
— What opportunities are there for providing the type of time shaping our customers want?
— What time distortions do we need to avoid?

Finding answers to these questions will present new opportunities for product/service design, marketing and, above all, enhanced customer care. What follows is a lead into answering these questions on a broad front. More detailed analysis for specific industries will be found in the Appendix.

14.4   OPPORTUNITIES IN THE PSYCHIC TIME-ZONES

Every industry operates in a dominant zone; many are also involved in tangential zones. As we have seen in Chapter 11, airlines primarily serve the travel needs of customers but to ensure customer satisfaction they have had to identify opportunities in terms of the biological, leisure, work and provisioning needs of passengers.

While it is relatively easy to identify the dominant zone, related zones will call for the ability to anticipate trends in customer needs. Table 14.1 summarises major consumer trends for the 1990s revealed by market research reports and surveys by major business magazines such as *Fortune, Management Today* and *Business Week*. Against each trend I have listed the most relevant psychic time-zones. By this means it is possible to identify the types of companies which will benefit from opportunities developing in each of the zones.

These broad trends will give rise to new markets for services and products which customers associate with particular psychic time-zones. Examples of these are given in Table 14.2.

Identifying the critical psychic time-zones of customers is dependent on:

- Market research
- Feedback on such questions as
  - 'What more can we do for you?'
  - 'What do you like best/least in the service we provide?'

The relative importance of particular psychic time-zones varies, not only between customers but at different stages in the life of any individual customer. All individuals however, experience effective or ineffective care in each of the groups of psychic time-zones described in Chapters 10 to 13:

- Life style zones
- Life work zones
- Passage of time zones (including the biological zone)

By identifying social, economic, political and technological trends associated with each of these groups it is possible to anticipate changing needs and expectations, not only in terms of 'customers' but in the many other roles – citizens, parents, employees, employers – which shape our perceptions and frame our priorities. Examples of these world-wide trends are listed in Table 14.3.

14.5 OPPORTUNITIES TO COMPETE *WITH* TIME

No matter the psychic time-zone they are in, there will be increased opportunities to help customers shape their time by bringing into play

continued on p. 244

Table 14.1 Customer-time-care opportunities in the 1990s

Consumer trend	Relevant psychic time zones	Companies benefiting from the trends
More time devoted to family and home	Family	Manufacturers of consumer durables and food
More time on healthy pursuits	Leisure Biological	Entertainment providers Medical care providers Health foods and drinks
Extend the life of raw materials through recycling	Durability	Packaging Waste disposal Publishers
More time on religious matters	Worship	Clothing manufacturers
A return to traditional designs	Chronological	Retailers
Making the best use of time	Work Travel Provisioning Communications Family	Most industries and services
More automation in the home		Computer manufacturers

Table 14.2   New markets for customer-time-care

BIOLOGICAL ZONE

Services	*Products*
Adult care	Physical supports
– Homes	Walking aids
– Nursing Homes	Wheelchairs
– Hospitals	Incontinent aids
	Strong flavoured, easily digested foods
Baby 'mirroring' to meet needs of 'old old'	
Energy conservation	Air conditioners
	CFC free energy conversion products
Alcohol substitution	Non-alcoholic beverages
Allergy prevention	Anti-air pollutants
Biotechnology	Waste disposal aids
Dental care	Dental products for the 'old old'
	Dental equipment for the 'old old'
Alternative medicine	Herbal products
	'New Age' treatments
Energy medicine	Advanced X Rays
	Scanners
Dieting services	Low fat foods
	Automatic calorie controllers
Exterminator services	Non-toxic products and techniques
Eye care	Products to prevent/control
	– Cataracts due to old age and ultra violet rays
	– Eyestrain due to video usage
	– Eye problems from air pollution
	Glasses
	Contact lenses
Pollution control	Filters for air/water
Hospitals	Medicines
	All medicinal aids
Death preparation services	Financial policies
	Cemetery security
	Personalised coffins
Hair fashioning	Hair preserving, shaping and colouring products
	Wigs
Mental health services	Brain scanners
Nutritional services	'Whole foods'
	Age-related foods
	Lifestyle foods

continued on p. 240

Table 14.2 *continued*

Orthopaedic services	Walking aids
	Special shoes
Skin care	Skin care products
Solar energy services	Solar heat capture and conserving products
Vitamin advice services	Vitamin pills/drinks
	Food supplements
Water services	Water conservators
	Water-recycling
	Water purifiers
	Bottled water

CHRONOLOGICAL ZONE

Services	*Products*
Astrological services	Personal horoscope predictors
	Books and videos on astrology in business
Photographic services	Cameras
	Film
Arts and crafts fairs	Aging aids
Antiques	Replicas
Museums	Preservation aids
Theme parks	Safe rides

COMMUNICATIONS ZONE

Services	*Products*
Cable television	Fee collection devices
	High-definition TV
	Transferable viewing devices
Computer services	All computer based or computer assisted products
Copying centres	Photocopiers
	Fax machines
Courier services	Secure vehicles
	Theft proof devices
Interpreter services	Automatic interpreters
Mail services	Greeting cards
	'Surprise' packages
Mobile telephone services	Mobile telephones
	Video phones
Magazines	Specialist publications
Speciality printing	Printing equipment
Video Conferencing	Video equipment

Table 14.2   *continued*

FAMILY ZONE

Services	Products
Adult home care	Easy to use products
	Convenience foods for 'old old'
	Lightweight appliances
Baby care	Nutritious foods
	Bio-degradable disposable clothes
Child-day care	Educational toys
Birthing services	Midwifery aids
Private education	Educational aids
Financial planning	Life-time financial products
Home extension	Greenhouses
	Mobile homes
Gardening services	Gardening tools for the old
Time compressing services	Microwave ovens
	Convenience foods
Insulation services	Heat-saving blinds

LEISURE ZONE

Services	Products
Vacation planning	Mobile products
	Aircraft
	Motor coaches
	Mobile hotels
	Cruise ships
	Adventure holidays
Cafes and restaurants	Coffee-making equipment
	Specialist restaurants
	Theatre restaurants
Camping services	Tents
	Mobile homes
Recreation	Power assisted
	– golf
	– tennis, etc.
Pet care services	Kennels, stables
	Pet foods
	Home aquariums
Cinema clubs	
Theatre clubs	
Home entertainment	
Party planning	
'Rest cure' resorts	
High risk sports	

Table 14.3   World-wide trends affecting perceptions and priorities

Passage-of-time zones	
Biological zone	Increased longevity
	Improved transplant surgery
	Concern re AIDS
	Growth of 'New Age' foods and medicines
Chronological zone	Growth in commemorative events
	Growth in theme parks/museums
	Decline in fashion?
	'Healthy clothes' moving into the biological zone
Durability zone	Growth in recycling
	Return of make do and mend philosophy
	Death of designed obsolescence
Global zone	Growth of 'time consciousness'
	Speeding up of delivery processes
	Charging for services by smaller time units
Lifework time zones	
Travel zone	Decline in time allocated to work journeys
	Payment for journey times related to work
	Growth of shared travel
Work zone	Reduction in time spent working by many; increase in time spent working by thrusting few
	Basis of pay moves from time to results
	Growth of flexi-time working
	Growth of 'shamrock' companies
Provisioning Zone	Reduction in time spent on essentials
	Discretionary buying melds with leisure zone
	'Open all hours' concept spreads
Communication zone	Growth in 'instant contact'
	Spread of tele-conferencing
	Growth of bi-location aids
Lifestyle time zones	
Family zone	Growth of vicarious contact
	Growth of carers
	Change in work/family balance
	Growth in new family-based celebrations
Leisure zone	Growth in participation
	Spread of healthy pursuits
	Increased theatre going
	Growth of exotic vacations
	Growth in potential development pursuits

Table 14.3   *continued*

Private zone	Emphasis on protecting privacy
	Growth of 'psychic' opportunities to 'get away from it all'
	Growth of 'exclusive' living and recreational facilities
Ritual zone	Growth of 'traditions' and special occasions
	Increased awareness of etiquette
	Spread of new 'international groupings' with distinctive protocols
Survival zone	Growth of security services
	Spread of 'safety consciousness'
	Decline in tolerance for 'abusers' of all types
	Growth of hedonic damages as well as physical injury claims
	Stricter conditions on drivers and others operating potentially lethal devices
Waiting zone	Decline in tolerance for waiting
	Growth of anticipating events
	Spread of 'leaks'
	Growth of 'instant' everything
Worship zone	Realignment of allegiances increases
	Increased involvement of lay people
	Growth of 'New Age' sects.

Table 14.4   Future trends influencing time shapers

Compressing	Will increase with improved automation and spread of 'instant gratification' syndrome
Layering	Will increase as with 'compressing' plus enhanced education and physical capabilities.
Diverting	Will grow as boredom threshold falls and exploitation of sensory perceptions increases.
Smoothing	Will increase in response to greater volatility in markets of all sorts
Substituting	Will increase with a decreasing tolerance for performing chores and the growth of quotidian services
Plexing	Will increase with the rise in cost of labour and other resources
Contra-flowing	Will increase as nostalgia spreads among old, and novelty syndrome grows at all ages
Extending	Will increase as desire grows for 'the personal touch' and a refuge from the frenetic

continued on p. 244

Table 14.3　*continued*

Exchanging	Will grow with increased specialisation and a growth of community spirit
Pacing	Will increase with greater interchange between cultures, the growth of the 'old old' and the 'differently abled'
Enhancing	Will increase with awareness of customer-time-care as a competitive weapon
Signalling	Will increase with growth of consumer assertiveness and penalties for default stemming from consumer biased legislation.

the techniques outlined in Chapters 8 and 9. A summary of the impact on time shapers of the trends already listed is given in Table 14.4.

Not all the twelve time shapers listed will be applicable to every industry, but considering them for each customer segment will provide fresh insights into how to compete *with* time rather than against time.

Time is infinite in its span. Customer-time-care is infinite in its opportunities. By grasping such opportunities and shaping them into distinctive patterns of customer-time-care, companies will become more competitive, more profitable and, above all, more caring.

Appendix: Putting the Concepts to Work

INTRODUCTION

In this part of the book you will find a variety of industry analyses and guides on implementing the concepts of customer care described in Parts I and II. The various analyses can be adapted by any company which seeks competitive advantage through customer care. At the end of this section is a glossary of terms used in customer-time-care.

CUSTOMER-TIME-CARE ANALYSIS OF BANKS

Banks are time-compressors. By lending money to an individual they enable him or her to acquire a physical asset or undertake a course of action which would otherwise be delayed to a later time. By providing opportunities to save and receive a rate of interest in so doing, banks enable the saver to accumulate wealth at an earlier time than would otherwise be the case. Finally, by transferring money from one location to another, banks enable financial transactions to be completed in a shorter time.

From time immemorial some individuals have had more of a particular commodity than they want, others have had less. The mechanism for creating a better balance between the 'haves' and the 'have nots' was barter, whereby goods of one type were exchanged for another. Barter determined the original 'time exchange balance'. However, it constrained the mobility of man to move between time-zones. Most of life was spent in a restricted section of the work time-zone.

This led to a search for a commonly acceptable commodity which would permit more complex time-exchange bargains to be effected – money. In order to secure the value of money it was made of precious metal, giving it a high value to weight and thus making it readily transportable.

The first known coins date from 650 BC and were used in Lydia in western Turkey. They were carefully weighed and had marks on the face which testified to their weight. This reduced the time-consuming practice of weighing coins at every transaction. It is the first example of building time-compression into a product. The result was that people saved time by accepting the coins at their face value. The use of pieces of metal with designated values imprinted on them continues to the present day.

However, most business transactions are conducted not in coin or paper currency but in 'financial instruments' which are accepted by bankers across the globe.

Banking is believed to have existed in Babylon and was thriving in the Roman Empire centuries before the birth of Christ. Romans used 'letters of credit' as did the Chinese as early as 900 BC. With the fall of the Roman Empire, banks declined in Europe until the thirteenth century when the Renaissance revitalised trading by the Italians. These Italian banks which prospered through three centuries provided the models for modern commercial banks. Banking did not take hold in the rest of Europe until the seventeenth century when banks were founded in the Netherlands, Sweden and England. The English banks were established by London goldsmiths.

Initially the goldsmiths used their secure vaults to store customers' valuables. A receipt was issued for each valuable and could be subsequently passed back to the customer when the valuable was redeemed. In due course, the receipts were recognised as a means of exchange, eliminating the time-consuming practice of having to visit the vaults and redeem a valuable for transfer. By 1668 Samuel Pepys was recording the use of this new 'bank note' by his father.

With the growth of industry and international trade, banks spread rapidly throughout the eighteenth and nineteenth centuries. In terms of customer-time-care the most significant banking development of the nineteenth century was the cheque – this commonly used bill of exchange made payments easier between people in different areas. It is being superceded in personal transactions by the plastic card and automatic teller machines.

The plastic card provides a variety of customer-time-care opportunities:

- As a credit card it provides the opportunity to purchase goods or services, delaying the time by which payment has to be made.
- As a charge card it provides a rotating opportunity to purchase goods or services, making payment in full by a specific date.
- As a debit card it reduces the time between making a purchase and paying for it, without having to carry cash around.
- As a transaction card it enables a range of financial services to be accessed at virtually any time without having to visit a particular bank.

PSYCHIC TIME-ZONES

Banks operate primarily in the work psychic time-zone, but are also involved with customers in the family psychic time-zone. The same individual may well be a customer in both zones. However, banks are tending to reduce 'zone confusion' by providing separate branches for dealing with business and personal matters at all levels.

Work Time-zone

In this zone opportunities to enhance customer-time-care will include:

— Meeting customer deadlines.
— Avoiding reworking due to errors.
— Anticipating customer problems and dealing with them in timely fashion.

— Compressing time in decision-taking on credit requests.
— Extending time to reschedule or otherwise change credit arrangements.

Family Time Zone

In this zone opportunities to enhance customer-time-care will include:

— Providing sufficient time to understand the total family circumstances.
— Pacing appropriate to life change, life enhancement and life maintenance needs.
— Automating services to improve time-compression.
— Extending time-layering. (For example, Japanese banks provide blood pressure measurement for older customers and the service of an astrologer.)

CUSTOMER-TIME-CARE ANALYSIS OF HOTELS

Hotels were devised to provide food, shelter and security for travellers. Their initial form was an inn. They were sources of income for government through collecting duties on alcohol and tobacco; as a result they have, from early times, been subject to licences and government inspection.

Inns continued to be the dominant provider of transitory accommodation until the late eighteenth century when the restorative powers of spas were sought by the aristocracy of England and Europe, particularly in Germany and Switzerland. This gave rise to the 'grand hotels' and made them providers of leisure, designed to pamper the self-indulgent.

The growth of railways in the nineteenth century spurred on the development of 'commercial hotels' designed to provide living accommodation and a work base for travelling salesmen. While capital cities and centres of industry possessed hotels of all types by the beginning of the twentieth century, it was not until the latter half of that century that 'hotel resorts' proliferated where there was sun, sand and sea. The growth of 'packaged holidays' gave birth in many countries to hotels as entertainment centres. This phenomenon continues with the development of Disneyland and other theme parks which have hotels linked to them.

A further development has been the use of hotels for wedding receptions and meetings of exclusive groups. Thus the hotel industry operates in several psychic time-zones:

(a) Leisure
(b) Work
(c) Family
(d) Ritual
(e) Biological

Each psychic time-zone provides opportunity for customer-time-care. Whichever the zone, there are a number of critical time-care pointers to be observed:

Arrival and check-in facilities must be smooth running. Customer anxiety surrounds such items as:

— Booking has been received.
— Accommodation is available.
— Access to room or optional facilities for refreshing oneself, leaving luggage and resting are hassle free.
— Room service is prompt.
— Check-out is swift.
— There are no disturbances.
— There is an awareness of teamwork.
— What's promised is delivered.

Leisure Psychic Time-zone

The essentials of customer-time-care in this zone are:

• Provide options of service provider planned time (such as games, cocktail parties, dances) *vis-à-vis* self-planned time.
• Identify opportunities to elongate time in terms of pleasure pursuits, e.g. offer 'extra time' for games rides, boutique opening hours.
• Provide opportunities for time contraflowing, particularly with meals, e.g. 'any time' breakfast; twenty-four-hour room service; permanently opened sports facilities. Golf, tennis, or other ball games using fluorescent balls and 'personal lighting systems' enable customers to extend play time.

Work Psychic Time-zone

The essentials of customer-time-care in this zone are:

• Effective communications within and outside the hotel.
• Flexibility in scheduling breaks.
• Strict time-keeping in providing meals.
• Ready access to business bureau services.

Family Psychic Time-zone

The essentials of customer-time-care in this zone are:

• Security and well-being of old/young dependants.
• Flexibility in timing and constitution of meals.
• Availability of basic medical and health related products, e.g. nappies, zimmer frames.
• Swift cleaning of any mess in the room.
• Secure and sensitive baby/old person monitoring systems.

Ritual Psychic Time-zone

The essentials of customer-time-care in this zone are:

- Privacy and security of clothes and insignia.
- Confidentiality which respects rituals and unusual behaviour.
- Specialist advice on matters of protocol.
- Ability of serving staff to be present when required and otherwise absent, but readily available.
- No interruptions due to clearing tables, pouring wine, opening/shutting doors at inappropriate times.
- Clear signage to private rooms.
- Standby support should things go wrong.

Biological Psychic Time-zone

The essentials of customer-time-care in this zone are:

- Hygiene in all places and activities.
- Choice of meals for all ages, diets and most common nationalities using the hotel.
- Optional health foods.
- Comfortable beds.
- Effective air conditioning.
- Adequate supplies of hot/cold water.

CUSTOMER-TIME-CARE GUIDELINES

Accountancy Services

Dominant psychic time-zone:	Work
Time-shaping techniques:	Time-compression – completing statutory accounts in less time than the customer. Time-layering – providing business guidance as well as financial services. Time-smoothing – enabling client to spread tax and other payments over a period.
Time-warp dangers:	Failing to comply with tax law which results in prosecution of client.

Dominant mindsets of clients:

Life change – resulting from significant change in financial situation.
Life enhancement – resulting from optimum use of tax avoidance schemes.
Life maintenance – seeking help with completion of routine tasks.

Special points:

In tax matters, accountants can be 'positive procrastinators' by enabling the client to postpone payment of taxes until the final deadline, without antagonising the revenue officials, nor incurring interest charges by the Inland Revenue which offsets any financial advantages arising from delayed payment.

Airports

Dominant psychic time-zone:

Waiting

Related psychic time-zones:

Travel, leisure, provisioning, communicating, work.

Time-shaping techniques:

Time-compression – reducing time spent waiting to check in, collect luggage, eat, get information, undergo security checks.
Time-layering – providing opportunities for shopping, entertainment, reading, meditating (in a special room), eating.
Diversion – reducing the negative impact of waiting by providing a range of activities which enable the customer to 'pass the time' enjoyably.

Time-warp danger:

Aircraft crash.

Dominant mindset of customer:

Airport customers fall into three categories:

– Passengers
– Greeters
– Spectators

The dominant mindset of passengers may be:

- Life change – individuals emigrating, attending a funeral, moving to a new job or getting married.
- Life enhancement – holidaying.
- Life maintenance – routine business travel, returning from holiday.

The dominant mindset of 'greeters' may be:

- Life change – seeing off a loved one; greeting a fellow mourner.
- Life maintenance – collecting an individual to take them to their ultimate destination.

The dominant mindset of spectators is:

- Life enhancement – they are using the airport as a 'leisure centre'.

Special points:

Most airport customers would rather be elsewhere; for them the airport is simply a waiting room. The negative time spent waiting can be alleviated by providing:

- Congenial lounges.
- Reliable and user-friendly information systems.
- Reasonably priced bars, restaurants and shops.
- Adequate telephones.
- Well-kept toilet facilities, including showers and changing rooms.
- Quiet areas.
- Reasonably priced television or film shows.

In terms of time-compression the layout should be designed to enable the time from curb to plane and vice versa to be very short. Clear

signage, with adequate
'reassurance' signs of staff, is very
important.

Antique Dealers

Dominant psychic time-zone: Chronological

Related psychic time-zone: Leisure

Time-shaping techniques: Time compression – acquiring an
                                   art work more quickly than the
                                   customer would be able to.
                                   Time-plexing – advising a customer
                                   on making an acquisition which will
                                   provide both pleasure and profit.
                                   Time-layering – Providing lectures
                                   and refreshments. Providing
                                   assistance in financing acquisitions.

Time-warp dangers: Fakes resulting in both psychic and
                                   financial damage to customers.
                                   Breakages resulting in financial
                                   loss.

Dominant mind-set of customers: In a selling mode customers may be
                                   in any of the three states:
                                   Life changing – having to sell due
                                   to death of another.
                                   Life enhancement – having to sell
                                   to acquire a more preferred object.
                                   Life maintenance – having to sell in
                                   order to meet normal commitments
                                   or provide more space.

                                   In the buying mode customers will
                                   generally be in the life-
                                   enhancement mindset.

Special points: Customers need time to browse,
                                   reflect and bargain. The provision
                                   of refreshments and a relaxing
                                   ambience can be useful in retaining
                                   the presence of Customers.

Bars and Cafés

Dominant psychic time-zone: Leisure

Related psychic time-zones:	Biological, waiting
Time-shaping techniques:	Time-elongating – sustaining a sense of relaxation and socialising. Time-layering – providing newspapers, meals and games.
Time-warp dangers:	Drunkenness and disorderly behaviour which affects both those directly involved and others.
Dominant mindset of customers:	Life enhancement – people go to bars to enjoy themselves; any factor which counters this causes negative time-states which will result in a loss of custom.
Special points:	Sale of alcohol is usually only allowed by law at prescribed times. Care should therefore be taken to avoid abrupt ending of service to comply with the law. Early warning systems and even making clocks register a later time than is the case are useful devices for helping customers to make a smooth transition from the leisure time-zone to the travel time-zone.

Cleaning Services

Dominant psychic time-zone:	Durability
Related psychic time-zones:	Biological
Time-shaping techniques:	Time-displacement – allows customer to use time saved in cleaning. Time-compression – completes cleaning in less time than customer would. Time-layering – opportunities to decorate premises and/or monitor security.
Time-warp dangers:	Theft resulting from inadequate security procedures. Breakages.

Dominant mindset customer:	Life maintenance
Special point:	Dry cleaners, laundries and other types of cleaning services must produce a significant time exchange premium since most customers perceive that they could perform the services for themselves if 'they had the time'. Added-value through innovative packaging, fast service and a clear indication of improved cleanliness are essential for assuring the customer of value for money and reducing guilt feelings about avoiding chores.

Courier Services

Dominant psychic time-zone:	Communications
Related psychic time-zone:	Waiting
Time-shaping techniques:	Time-compressing – transporting items swiftly from one location to another.
Time-warp danger:	Loss of items in transit.
Dominant mindset of customers:	Mainly life maintenance, but can be life change (transport of medicine and organ transplants) or life enhancement (transport of gifts).
Special points:	The customer uses courier services for both speed and security; another important factor is reassurance that an item has been delivered in good time. Added value can be provided through telephoning or faxing the sender confirmation of delivery.

Estate Agency Services

Dominant psychic time-zone:	Family
Related psychic time-zone:	Waiting
Time-shaping techniques:	Time-compression – enhances chance of finding appropriate

	property in a short time. Time-layering – can help on related issues such as mortgages, insurance, furniture purchase, painting and decorating, social contacts.
Time-warp danger:	Purchase/sale falls through at last moment.
Dominant mind-set of customer:	Life change – considerable emotional investment in any house move. Can distort perceptions of role of the estate agent.
Special points:	House selling and purchase is a time-consuming and emotionally demanding business much of which is in the waiting zone. The essential of customer-time-care is to minimise the time spent in that zone by:

- Providing realistic expectations to the vendor.
- Ensuring that purchasers are guided towards realistic prospects.
- Anticipating customers' needs for specialist services.
- Being contactable at virtually any time.
- Having ready access to a range of services which are expert at time-compression.

Fashion Retail

Dominant psychic time-zone:	Chronological
Related psychic time-zone:	Biological
Time-shaping techniques:	Time compression – providing a complete wardrobe and accessories at 'one stop'. Time-contraflowing – making the individual appear younger/ slimmer/taller/smaller.
Dominant mindset of customer:	Life enhancement – individual wants to establish or reinforce a positive self-image.

(Life change will be relevant for wedding outfits.)

Special points:

Fashion clothes are for satisfying psychic needs rather than physical needs. Fashion is therefore associated with the chronology of time, rather than with protecting the body. Since selecting fashion clothes is a life-enhancing activity the customer should feel relaxed when making a choice. Once an initial offer of help is made the retailer should stay discreetly in the background. The offer of help should be couched in terms of an option – 'Would you prefer to browse or would you like some help?'

Comments on choices should focus on self-image (if positive) or on the clothes, if negative. For example:

- 'You look so at ease in that suit – it's just you.'
- 'That dress is too short/ long/big/small. It doesn't do you justice.'

Purchasers of fashion clothes want to feel that they are abreast of the times, even ahead of it. The use of video displays of current fashion can stimulate the buying decision. Where customers are over 50 the models displaying the fashions should be ten years younger.

Funeral Services

Dominant psychic time-zone: Ritual

Related psychic time-zone: Family, biological, private, travel

Time-shaping techniques: Time compression – coordinating a range of legal, religious and medical requirements.
Time-contraflowing – enhancing the appearance of a corpse.

Dominant mindset of customer:

Life change – customer may be 'in shock' and will need patient, sensitive handling.

Special points:

Funeral directors need to be able to:

- Obtain death certificates.
- Provide coffin (and sometimes pall bearers).
- Place death notice in newspapers.
- Provide embalming services.
- Arrange burial or cremation.
- Transport corpse and mourners to funeral.

In pursuing these activities, the funeral director is operating in a variety of time-zones while the customer may be 'stuck' in the ritual time-zone in a state of grief. This can lead to misunderstandings and customer perceptions of 'poor service'. One of the time skills of a funeral director is to coordinate activities swiftly while appearing to move at a more measured pace when in the presence of the bereaved.

Funeral directors tend to be busier in winter than in summer and need to plan their resources accordingly.

Garages and Filling Stations

Dominant psychic time-zone:

Travel

Related psychic time-zones:

Durability, provisioning, biological

Time-shaping techniques:

Time-compression – enabling motorist to resume journey as soon as possible.
Time-layering – enabling motorist to stock up with provisions; eat, drink, use toilet facilities.

Dominant mindset of customer:

Life maintenance in most cases.
Life enhancement if buying a car.

Time-warp danger:	Fire, explosion due to fuel leakage or other cause.
Special points:	Whether seeking fuel or car repair and maintenance, customers seek minimal disturbance to their journey. The provision of a substitute car while another is being repaired or maintained is a significant added-value. Other examples of customer-time-care are:

- Pumps which provide fuel for fixed sums of money as well as in volume terms.
- Car cleaning while you eat or drink.
- Reminders of due dates for routine maintenance.
- Provision of hire of accessories such as roof racks and small trailers.
- Fixing of accessories.

Hairdressing

Dominant psychic time-zone:	Biological
Related psychic time-zones:	Leisure, chronological
Time-shaping techniques:	Time-layering – provision of manicures and pedicures; use of personal stereos. Time-compression – provision of service at home or work, reducing waiting time.
Dominant mindset of customer:	Life enhancement – if seeking a new hairstyle or preparing for a special event. Life maintenance – if controlling growth and keeping hair clean. (Life change may dominate if customer is seeking a hair transplant with other changes in mind.)
Time-warp danger:	Injury or spread of disease due to lack of hygiene.

Special points:	For many men hairdressing is primarily a chore undertaken for reasons of hygiene. For many women it is primarily a means of enhancing self-image. Therefore, men seek to spend less time in a hairdressing salon than women do (regardless of relative amounts of hair). Since a chore element is usually associated with hairdressing there is added-value in providing the services on the customers' premises either at home or at work.

Nursing Homes

Dominant psychic time-zone:	Biological
Related psychic time-zones:	Private, family, chronological, leisure
Time-shaping techniques:	Time-layering – providing a range of different services aimed at keeping customers interested and healthy. Time-compression – enabling customers to perform chores more quickly than they would without assistance.
Time-warp danger:	Suicide or accidental death arising from circumstances within the control of the nursing home.
Dominant mindset of customer:	Life change – during initial period in nursing home. Life maintenance – once settled in nursing home.
Special points:	Nursing homes for the elderly need to help their customers consciously move across time-zones. Otherwise, as people get older they tend to spend much time in the retro time-state, going back to earlier times. They also seek to remain for long periods in the private time-zone, becoming introspective and

unwilling to interact with others. Nursing homes must therefore pay increasing attention to caring for the psychic as well as the physical needs of their customers. In a sense, what may appear as leisure time to the providers of the service is perceived as 'ritual' time by the elderly – things to be done in a prescribed manner to satisfy certain traditions.

Perhaps of all service providers, those in nursing homes have the most difficult task in identifying the time care needs of their customers.

Restaurants

Dominant psychic time-zone:

Biological

Related psychic time-zones:

Leisure, work, ritual

Time-shaping techniques:

Time-compression – providing fast food where appropriate.
Time-plexing – providing opportunities for celebrating, conducting business, relaxing, holding rituals, family gatherings, as well as eating and drinking.

Dominant mindset of customer:

Type of meal will generally indicate mindset:
Wedding breakfast – life change
Candlelit dinner – life enhancement
Business lunch – life maintenance

Time-warp dangers:

Bad behaviour of staff or customer disturbs ambience.
Food poisoning.

Special points:

Restaurants can be divided into two categories:

– Eating centres
– Leisure centres.

In both cases it is important that the food served is fit for human consumption. Hence their customers, while eating, are in the biological time-zone. However, where a restaurant is perceived as a source of enjoyment as well as nourishment, customers are usually in a different time-zone psychologically as they satisfy their physical need for food. Many restaurants are in the entertainment business – 20 per cent food, 40 per cent atmosphere and 40 per cent hype.

Zoos and Theme Parks

Dominant psychic time-zone:	Leisure
Related psychic time-zones:	Family, chronological, waiting
Time-shaping techniques:	Time-plexing – offering opportunities for entertainment, education, celebration, family outings. Time-contraflowing – offering experiences of going back in time (in theme parks).
Dominant mindset of customer:	Life enhancement – most people visit zoos and theme parks for pleasure which is expected to last for the whole period of the visit.
Time-warp danger:	Injury arising from equipment or animals.
Special points:	The one time-zone which customers abhor in zoos and theme parks is waiting. Care needs to be taken to reduce waiting time by such means as:

- Timed tickets for popular events.
- Staggering of feeding times for animals.
- Diversions such as clowns to entertain people queuing.
- Provision of a number of alternative routes encompassing main attractions.
- Well-located eating and toilet facilities.
- Clear signage.

Zoos and theme parks are highly seasonal businesses. They also tend to be busiest at weekends. This offers opportunities to make the facilities available at quiet times for business conventions, outings by the old, etc.

Glossary

Biological time:	The psychic time-zone in which organisms are conceived, born, grow and die.
Chronological time:	The psychic time-zone in which an individual experiences the differing phases in the passage of time from the past through the present, to the future.
Communications time:	The psychic time-zone in which an individual strives to make others or another aware of his/her feelings, desires, reactions or aspirations.
Core time:	The irreducible period of time needed to provide a particular product or service.
Customer-time-care:	A range of techniques which aim at shaping the time of an individual in a manner which will optimise customer satisfaction with a product or service.
Dominant life-need:	A requirement by an individual of satisfaction of a perceived or actual need at a particular point in time.
Durability time:	The psychic time-zone in which individuals seek to preserve the longevity or effectiveness of a product.
Family time:	The psychic time-zone in which relationships between individuals are established and maintained by a sharing of kinship or mutual interest.
Global time:	The concept which provides accurate measurements for gauging the passage of time.
Leisure time:	The psychic time-zone in which individuals experience a passage of time which is shaped by them to provide optimum satisfaction, without recourse to the needs and expectations of others. (For example, going to a circus because

you enjoy it is leisure time; going because your children enjoy it is family time; going to review it as a newspaper reporter is work time.)

Life-changing mindset: A state of mind associated with a major transformation in the life of an individual.

Life-enhancing mindset: A state of mind associated with an improvement in the circumstances of an individual which is of limited duration.

Life-maintaining mindset: A state of mind associated with carrying out an activity which is necessary to sustaining life in a particular society.

Life-style time-zone: A psychic time-zone which impacts directly or individually on the lifestyle of an individual. There are six such zones: Family; Leisure; Private; Ritual; Work; Worship.

Life-work time-zone: A psychic time-zone which is occupied by individuals in pursuit of acquiring the means necessary to maintain or enhance their standard of living. There are four such zones: Communicating; Provisioning; Travelling; Working.

Negative time-state: A state of mind within a particular psychic time-zone which results in a loss or lessening of satisfaction by an individual, negatively influencing their perception of an experience in using a product or service.

Passage of time-zone: A psychic time-zone in which individuals experience a consciousness of the passage of time and its relationship to their circumstances at a particular point in time. There are two such zones: Chronological; Durable.

Peripheral time: Time involved in activities associated with the core time of a service or an event, e.g. waiting for an aircraft to take off.

Positive time-state: A state of mind within a particular

psychic time-zone which results in self-satisfaction by an individual and which positively influences their perception of an experience.

Private time:

The psychic time-zone in which an individual undertakes activities or undergoes experiences in self-imposed isolation from others.

Provisioning time:

The psychic time-zone in which an individual acquires what is physically necessary to sustain life to a specific standard.

Psychic time-zone:

A perception of time passing which encompasses related activities, events or feelings which are experienced at different points of global time, individually or with others.

Purchasable time:

A measurable period of time for which an individual purchases the services of another, so releasing that time for the purchaser to pursue other activities. Usually the period of purchasable time is less than it would take the purchaser to perform the activity if undertaken by self.

Ritual time:

The psychic time-zone in which individuals adhere to a specified sequence of actions which are recognised as appropriate to the consummation of a particular event.

Survival time:

The psychic time-zone in which all endeavours are focused on undergoing an experience with minimal adverse effects on life or limb.

Time-compressing:

A technique or device for increasing customer satisfaction by making available in a short period of time a range of experiences or reducing the time required to achieve a particular goal.

Time-contraflows:

A technique or device for increasing customer satisfaction by either extending product life or making a product available earlier than is the norm.

Time-displacing: A technique or device whereby a customer is able to enjoy an experience at a different point in global time from that at which the experience is taking place (e.g. a viewer in England watching a football game in Los Angeles being transmitted live).

Time disturbance: Activities within a time-zone which reduce the enjoyment of positive time-states.

Time diversion: A technique or device for diverting an individual from experiencing a negative time-state.

Time enhancement: A technique or device for embellishing or extending the positive time experience of customers.

Time-exchange balance: The matching of the outcome of time spent by an individual on one or more activities with the outcome of time spent by another individual (or individuals) on another activity. (For example, income received from producing a piece of equipment is exchanged for food.)

Time intrusion: Actions from another psychic time-zone which reduce the enjoyment of positive time-states.

Time-layering: A process whereby customer satisfaction is enhanced by the opportunity to experience the positive effects of being in more than one psychic time-zone within a specific period.

Time-plexing: A technique or device for a product or service which can be used simultaneously by customers each of whom is in a different psychic time-zone.

Time-smoothing: A technique for reducing the impact of fluctuations in demand for a product or service, thereby reducing the adverse effects of such fluctuations on customers receiving a particular product or service.

Time-state:	The state of mind which determines the perceptions and behaviour of an individual at any given instant in a psychic time-zone.
Time substitution:	Undertaking for payment an activity which would otherwise consume the time of the individual paying for the activity.
Travel time:	The psychic time-zone in which an individual is transported from one location to another.
Time-warps:	Sudden, unexpected changes of psychic time-zone which are outside the control of an individual and have a negative impact.
Universal or cosmic time:	The concept which determines the passage of time throughout the known Universe, with particular reference to the interaction of the planets.
Waiting time:	The psychic time-zone in which individuals experience a sense of holding on, anticipating or enduring a passage of time in order to acquire, experience or receive satisfaction from a particular event, or satisfy a need.
Work time:	The psychic time-zone in which individuals expend energy in the pursuit of activities which will enable them to exchange the output of their efforts for the acquisition of products and experiences which would otherwise be unattainable.
Worship time:	The psychic time-zone in which individuals seek to transcend more mundane experiences to communicate with a person or force in another existence or in an accentuated form.

Bibliography

Crosby, Philip B., *Let's Talk Quality* (McGraw-Hill, 1989).
Hawking, Stephen W., *A Brief History of Time* (Bantam Press, 1988).
International Management (July 1990).
Juran, J. M., *Juran on Quality Leadership* (Free Press, 1989).
Lynch, James J., *A Manpower Development System* (Pan Books, 1970).
Mella, Dorothee L., *The Language of Colour* (Michael Joseph, 1990).
Morris, Desmond, *Manwatching* (Jonathan Cape, 1977).
Porter, Michael E., *The Competitive Advantage of Nations* (Macmillan, 1990).
Signal International, 'The Invisible Consumer' (June 1990).
Time Magazine, Young Americans (July 1990).
Woolley, Benjamin, in *The Listener* (18 October 1990).

Index